Safe Family C

CW01478592

with

Windows Vista ™

Tony Loton

LOTONtech

www.lotontech.com

Contents

Acknowledgements

I'd like to thank all those who volunteered to review the original manuscript for this book; for no more reward than a mention here – and a copy of the book.

Special thanks go to John Leese (a lifelong friend, and fellow IT professional) and Debbie Loton (my company secretary, proof-reader... and wife).

About the author

Tony Loton is a Microsoft Certified Professional (MCP) who specializes in the latest Microsoft tools, techniques and technologies including Visual Studio Team System and Windows Vista.

Tony works through his company, LOTONtech Limited, as an independent consultant, trainer, and technical author. He has previously published IT books through Wrox Press and John Wiley & Sons, and has written feature articles for IT journals and the Microsoft MSDN web site.

Outside of IT, Tony has a keen interest in personal finance and financial trading. He also writes on those topics.

Introduction

This book is not for computer geeks.

It's for regular people such as parents, who have purchased one or more personal computers for the family and who are concerned about how those computers can be used safely on-line and off-line so that:

- Individual computer users – particularly children, maybe your granny, or even you – are protected from illegal, immoral, pornographic, or violent content.

- The computer itself is resilient to attack from viruses, spyware, and other malevolent forces resident on the Internet.

Personal Computers (PCs) are very powerful tools, but notoriously difficult for the average user to install, configure, and secure. This results in the majority of parents and other responsible adults simply letting their children set-up their own computers, remaining blissfully ignorant about how those computers are being used.

This book is primarily concerned with the family oriented security features of Windows Vista that contribute towards a safer computing environment for the whole family. Since your household will likely have additional computers running the older Windows XP, I also – where appropriate – make suggestions on how similar family safety features may be applied on those computers.

The prospect of configuring your Windows Vista computer for safe family computing might set you on fire with excitement. Don't worry, this book will simplify the process and the end result will be well worth the effort. Better safe than sorry!

Although I've not labeled the chapters specifically as ordered steps, there is some logic to the order in which I present the information.

As you read through the book you will notice that some elements of the text are shown as *Italic Text* or **Bold Text**. While occasionally this may be merely for emphasis, generally the convention is as follows:

Italic Text is for titles, labels, application names etc. that you see on the screen and which I show in figures (pictures).

Bold Text is for active buttons and links that you can **click** or otherwise interact with to perform some action.

In the figures, you will often see a *CLICK HERE* (CLICK HERE) indicator superimposed. This visual indication reinforces the instructions given in the text immediately preceding or following the figure. Try not to rush ahead and click until you've read the relevant instructional text.

That's all I need to say by way of introduction, and I wish you well in your endeavor to assure 'Safe Family computing with Windows Vista'.

Tony Loton, November 2007

1 – Windows Security Center

Objective: To check your computer's security settings.

As soon as your computer is connected up, and switched on for the first time, it's time to check the computer's security settings. It's not too late if you've been using your computer for a while, but you should do this as soon as possible – ideally, as the first thing you do after installation.

I'll show you how to check your computer's security settings using Windows *Security Center*.

This is perhaps the most technical chapter in the book; but in most cases you won't need to make any changes, and the default settings will suffice. Nonetheless it's worth taking the time to check that everything is as it should be.

Accessing Windows Security Center

First you need to launch the Windows *Control Panel* by clicking the Windows **Start** button (the flag symbol at the bottom left of your screen) followed by the **Control Panel** menu option. As shown here in Figure 1.

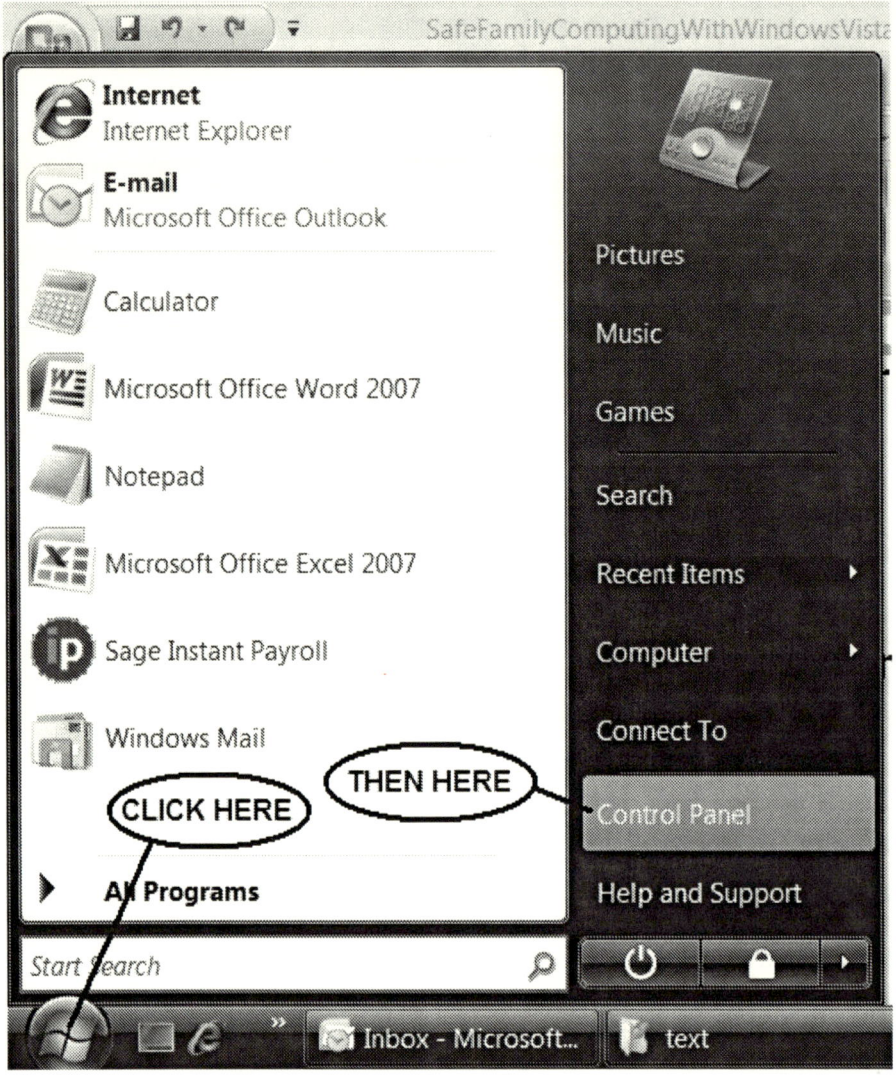

Figure 1 Launching Windows Control Panel

With Control Panel in *Classic View* you should select the
Security Center item as shown in Figure 2:

Safe Family Computing with Windows Vista

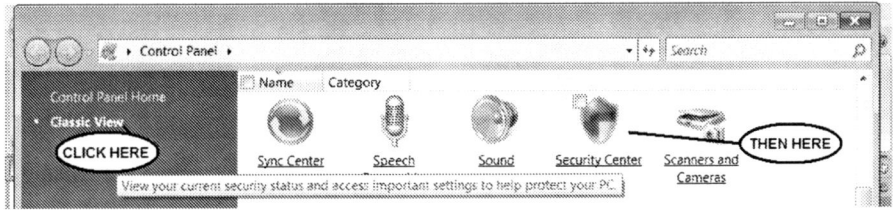

Figure 2 Security Center link in Control Panel Classic View

Alternatively, with Control Panel in *Control Panel Home* view you should select the **Check this computer's security status** link as shown in Figure 3:

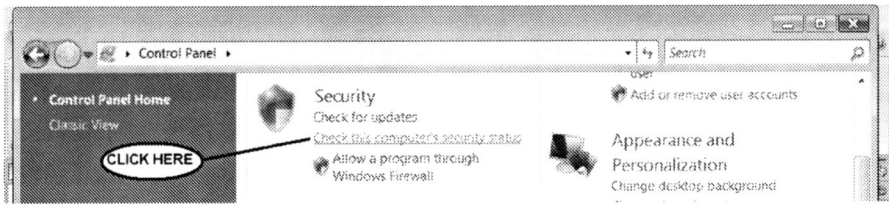

Figure 3 Check this computer's security status

The *Windows Security Center* is shown in Figure 4:

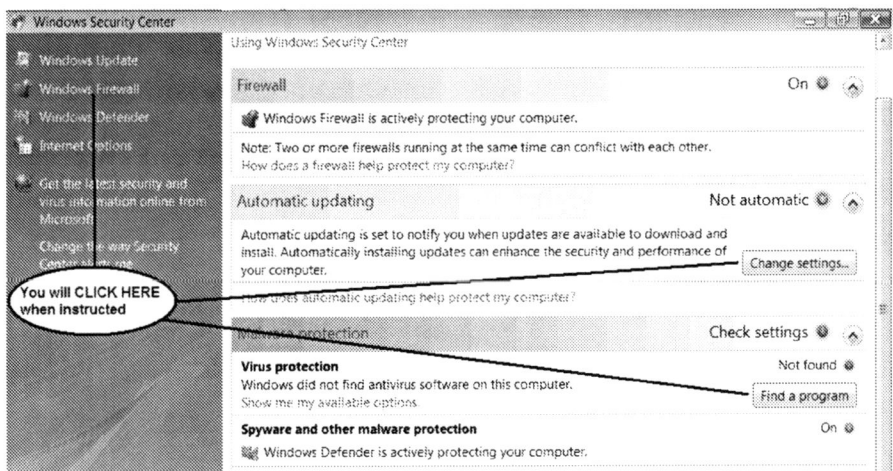

Figure 4 Windows Security Center

In Figure 4 I have expanded each of the three sections – *Firewall*, *Automatic updating*, and *Malware protection* – by clicking the arrow symbol ⊛ on each section.

You can see that my computer currently has *Firewall* switched *On*, *Automatic updating* switched on but *Not automatic*, and *Malware protection* flagged as *Check settings* (because I have Windows Defender, but no additional antivirus software).

Security Center components
Let's take each of those Security Center components in turn, starting with *Firewall*.

Firewall
The purpose of the Windows Firewall is to block unwanted data from flowing to and from your computer over the network; rather like locking your doors and windows, so that only people you trust can get in. It helps prevent people from remotely accessing and controlling your computer over the Internet, as well as helping to stop your computer connecting to other computers without your knowledge.

To access the firewall settings, select the **Windows Firewall** link shown in the top-left of Figure 4. Figure 5 shows what you will see:

Figure 5 Windows Firewall

I already have the firewall switched on (see above). If yours is not switched on, you should switch it on without delay. You can do that by clicking the **Turn Windows Firewall on or off** link, or by clicking the **Change settings** link.

You should first see the *User Account Control* dialog appear (not shown here), which states that *"Windows needs your permission to continue."*

You'll see that dialog regularly as you follow the steps in this book, and it's the way Windows Vista checks that the action has been performed by the person actually sitting at the computer screen. In the unlikely event that you ever see that dialog when you have not done anything yourself, select **Cancel**; but in this case press **Continue**.

The *Windows Firewall Settings* dialog (shown next) provides radio buttons to turn the firewall **On** (do it now) and **Off** (don't do it unless you really know what you're doing).

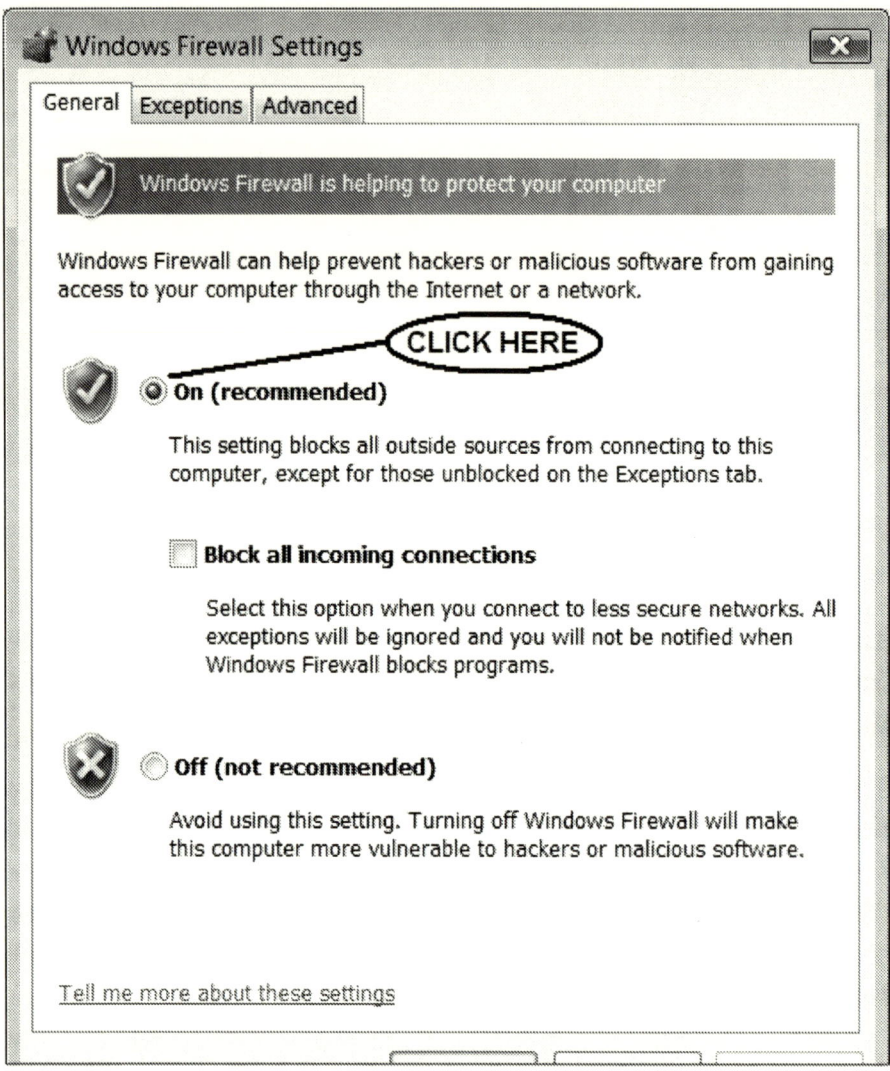

Figure 6 Windows Firewall Settings, General

In most cases you'll have to leave the **Block all incoming connections** box unchecked, as there will be some programs which you will want to have remote connections over the network.

To show you what those programs might be I have selected the **Exceptions** tab:

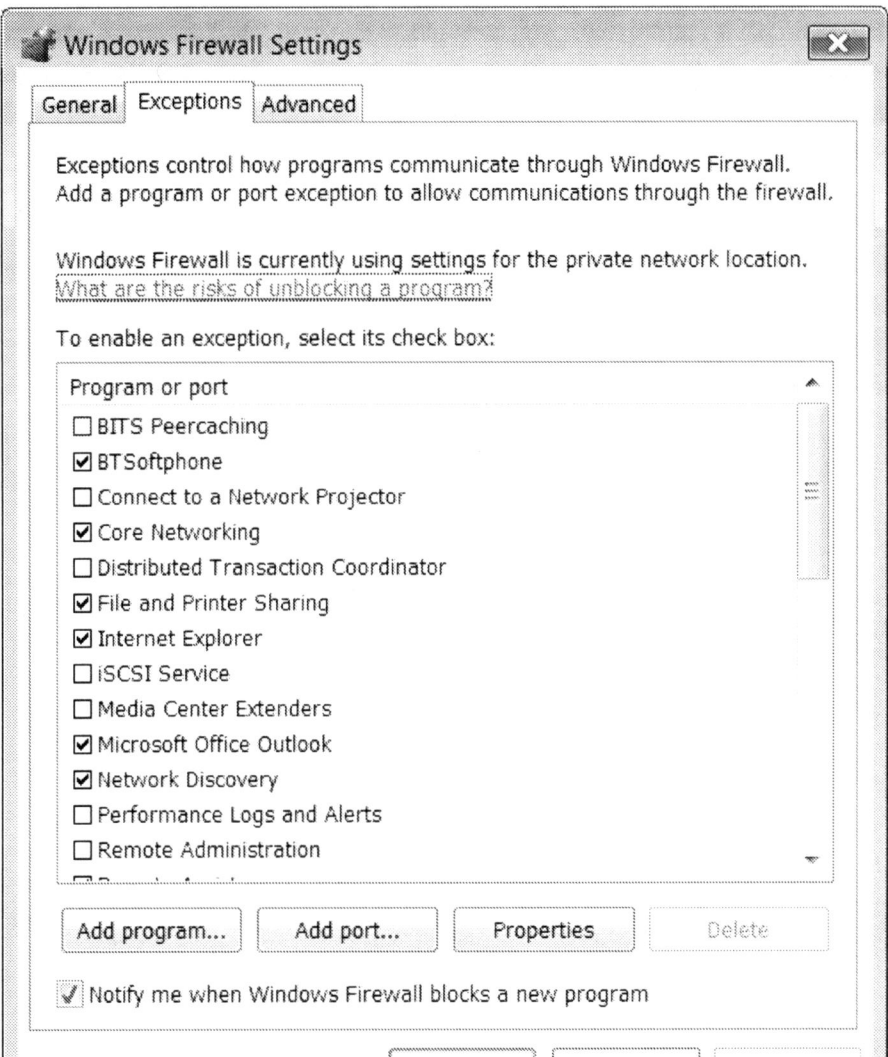

Figure 7 Windows Firewall Settings, Exceptions

You can see that my settings allow the firewall to be bypassed, for example, by **File and Printer Sharing** but not by **Remote Administration**.

I discourage you from checking and un-checking these boxes unless you know what you're doing. Chances are you won't need to, because Windows will prompt you to allow or block access to a program as necessary. For example, I never explicitly checked the box next to *BT Softphone*; it was added to the exceptions list as a consequence of me installing the software.

The final tab, marked **Advanced,** allows you to select which networks are secured by the firewall. I strongly recommend you enable the firewall for all network connections as I have below, unless – for example – you have a home network that will never connect outwardly to the Internet.

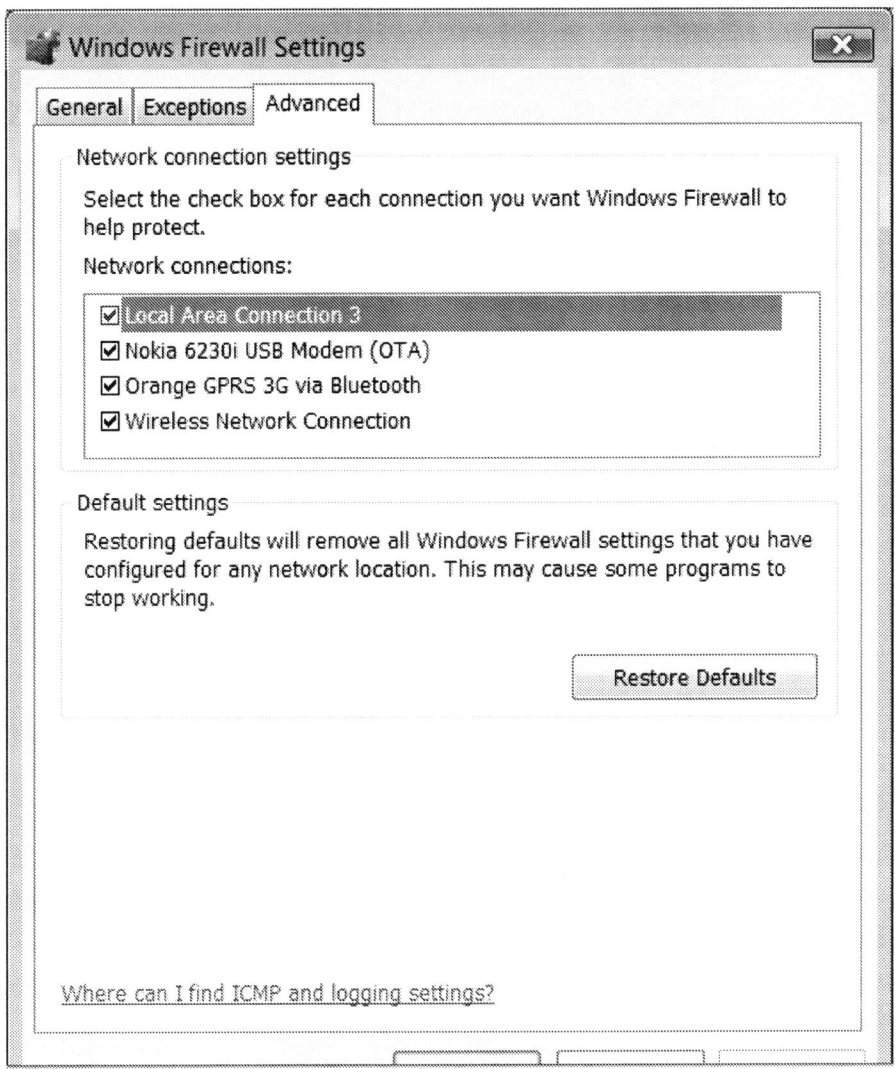

Figure 8 Windows Firewall Settings, Advanced

<u>Automatic updating</u>
The second Windows *Security Center* component (Figure 4) is **Automatic updating**. Windows updates are additions to software that can prevent or fix problems, enhance the security of the computer, or improve the computer's performance.

You can *Choose an automatic updating option* by pressing the **Change settings...** button on the *Windows Security Center* page (Figure 4). Figure 9 shows what you'll see.

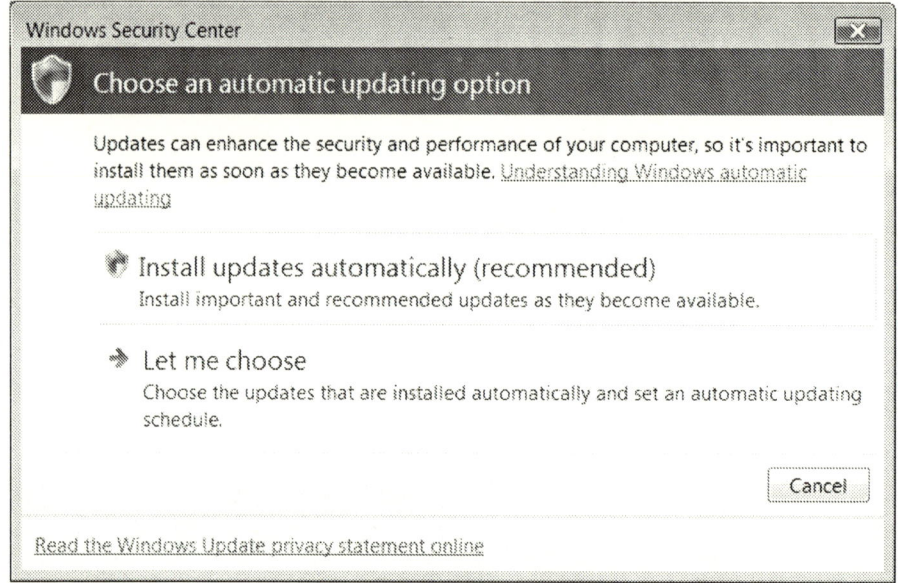

Figure 9 Choose an automatic updating option

As you see, the recommended option is to *Install updates automatically*. If you want a quiet life in which all your computer updates are downloaded and installed automatically behind the scenes, you should follow that recommendation.

Actually, I don't. And the reason is that automatic updates can occur frequently – which uses Internet connection bandwidth and can slow down the computer's performance while the automatic updating takes place.

I like to choose when updates are downloaded and installed, at a time convenient to me, by clicking the **Let me choose** link.

As you can see in Figure 10, I can choose from three possibilities: **Install updates automatically** (the recommended setting), **Download updates but let me choose whether to install them**, or **Check for updates but let me choose whether to download and install them** (my personal choice).

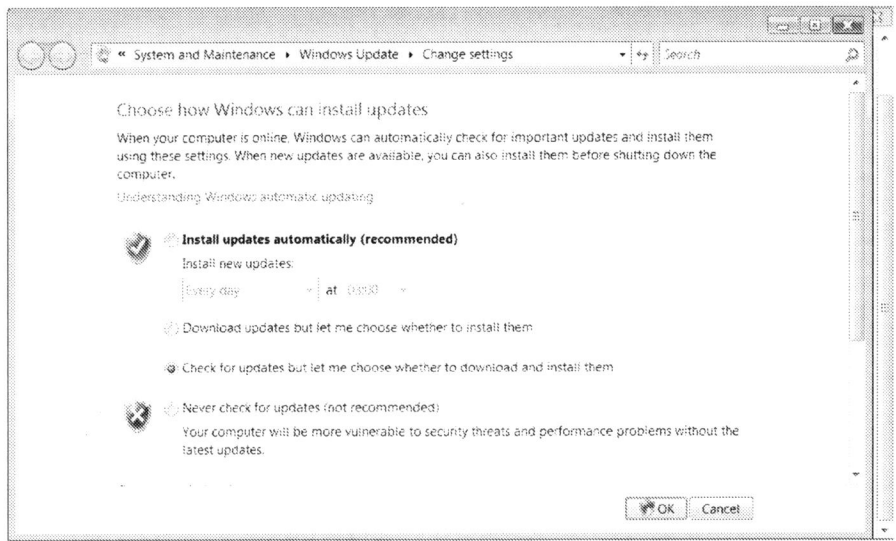

Figure 10 Windows Update, Change settings

Yes, I know there's a fourth choice – **Never check for updates** – but that's not recommended at all.

My computer checks periodically over the Internet to find out if any updates are available. If there are, I get prompted to download and install them; which I do, as I said, at a time convenient to me. Note that I am an IT professional and I'm disciplined enough to do that, but most people aren't (no offense!).

If you choose the same route as me, you may well receive more 'update' prompts than you expect. To give you an idea of how frequently these updates occur (without your intervention if you choose the automatic options) take a look at my update history in Figure 11.

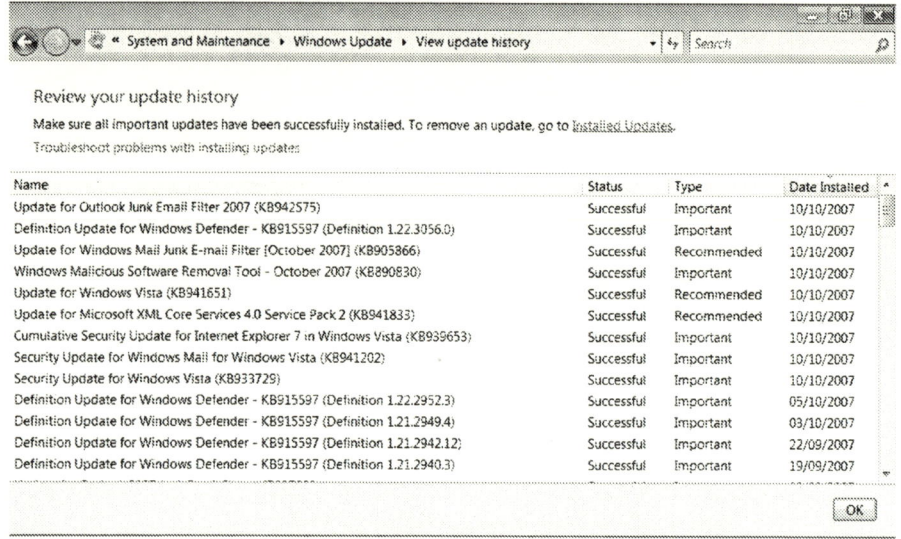

Figure 11 Windows Update, View update history

You can view your own update history, and perform other update functions, by selecting the **Windows Update** link on the *Windows Security Center* page (Figure 4). That will take you to the main Windows Update page, shown in Figure 12.

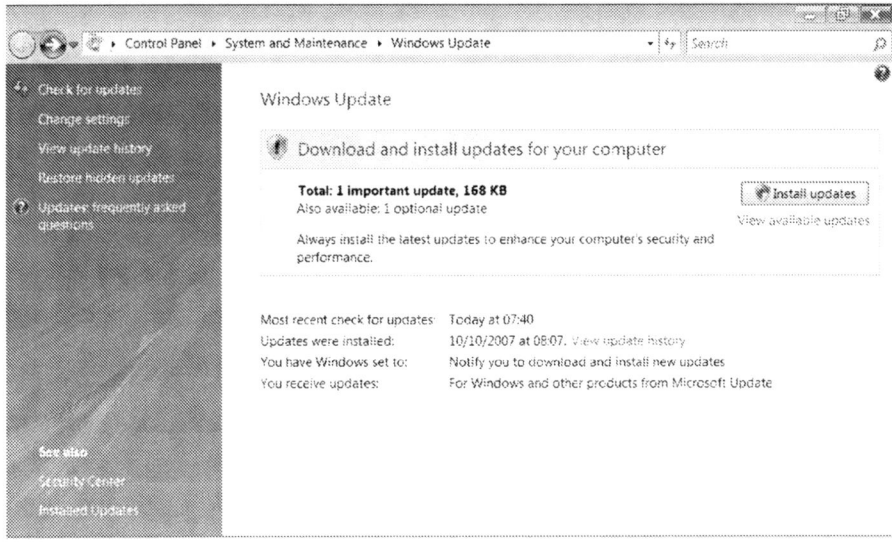

Figure 12 Windows Update

You can see here that I have some updates yet to install, and that from the links on the left I can **View update history**. I can also **Change settings** (already described, Figure 10), and **Restore hidden updates** (which are updates that I previously declined to install).

If all this seems complicated, don't worry. Just select the **Install updates automatically** link (Figure 9 or Figure 10) and forget all about it.

Malware Protection – AntiVirus

There are two kinds of malware (**mal**icious soft**ware**): *viruses* and *spyware*. In this section I'll consider viruses. These are potentially harmful programs that spread from computer to computer, rather like biological viruses spreading from person to person.

Looking back at Figure 4 (Security Center), you can see that I <u>do not</u> have virus protection installed. I wanted to show you that Windows Vista does not come with antivirus software as part of the package. You have to find your own! Your computer might have come bundled with free-trial antivirus software, or the computer salesman might have encouraged you to buy this software at the point of purchase. If not, you can find an antivirus program by clicking the **Find a program** button (shown in Figure 4). That takes you to the *Microsoft antivirus partners* web page, from where you can purchase a recommended program along with a subscription for antivirus updates.

Personally I'm not a big fan of third-party antivirus programs because they can sometimes interfere with the smooth running of Windows, especially when they come bundled with additional protection programs (such as firewall) that duplicate the Windows functionality.

If you find that your third-party antivirus software does turn out to be more hindrance than help, you might have to temporarily disable it or uninstall it. In which case you must take care to:

- Use the other Windows Security Center components to protect your computer from unauthorized remote access (protected by Firewall), known Windows security deficiencies (protected by Automatic Updates), and spyware (protected by Windows Defender, described next).

- Practice safe computing as described in Chapter 7 – Safe Computing Tips for Users, for example by not downloading software from dubious sources nor opening e-mail attachments from people you don't know.

Whatever antivirus protection program you choose, you'll have to refer to the provider's manual for further instruction. After all, I don't know which one you'll pick.

I look forward to the day that Microsoft bundles an antivirus program with Windows. In the meantime, they do offer the Windows Live OneCare as described in Appendix A – Windows XP Family Safety; which also provides antivirus protection for Windows Vista.

Malware Protection – AntiSpyware

As I said previously, there are two kinds of malware (**mal**icious soft**ware**): *viruses* and *spyware*. In this section I'll consider spyware. This is software that tracks a user's web browsing and other actions, and transmits that information to a potentially malicious third party.

The Windows Vista antispyware program is called *Windows Defender*.

You can launch *Windows Defender* from the *Windows Security Center* (Figure 4), or directly from the Windows *Start* menu as shown in Figure 13.

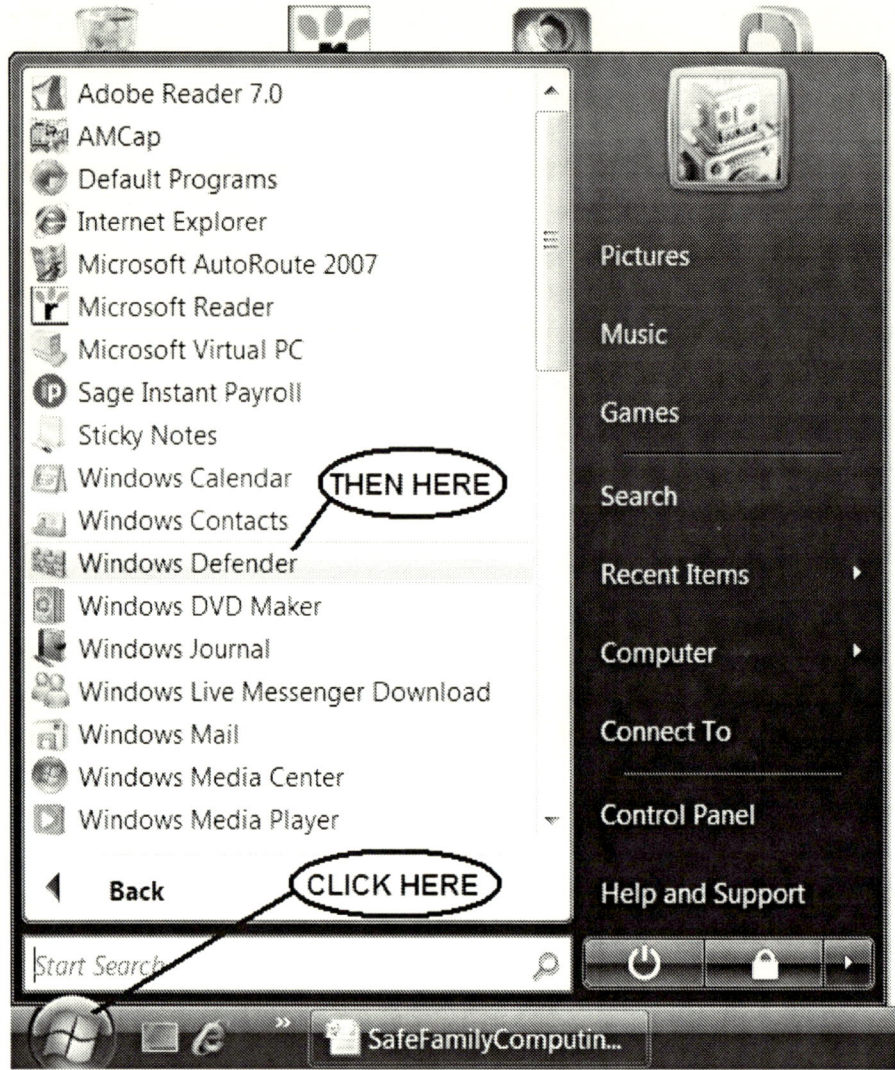

Figure 13 Launch Windows Defender from Start Menu

The most obvious function of Windows Defender is to scan your computer for potentially harmful programs. On the Windows Defender main screen, press the **Scan** button or choose your type of scan – **Quick Scan** or **Full Scan** – from the *Scan* pull-down menu like this:

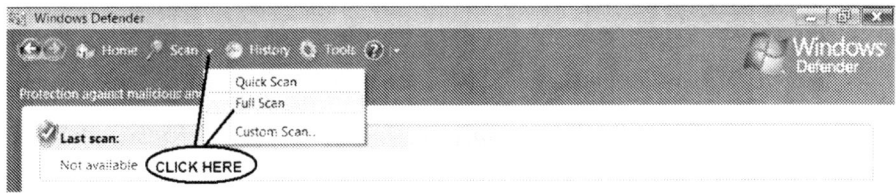

Figure 14 Windows Defender main page

Of course, that technique assumes that you will actually remember to press the **Scan** button at periodic intervals. All-the-better, then, that the process can be automated.

Select the **Tools** option from the menu bar and you will see the following screen:

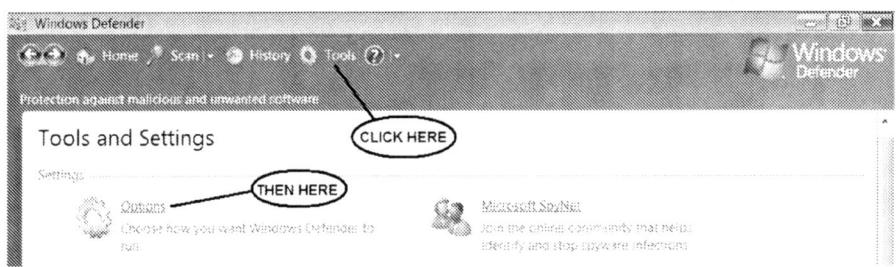

Figure 15 Windows Defender Tools and Settings

Click **Options** to launch the following screen which shows the *Automatic scanning* setting (Figure 16).

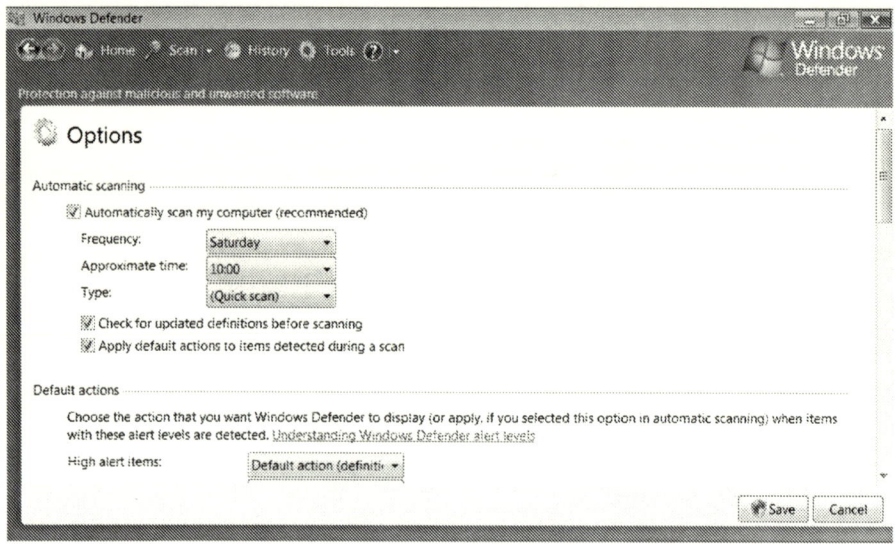

Figure 16 Windows Defender Options

By default the automatic scan will be set to run daily at approximately 2am (assuming your computer is switched on at that time). You can leave it alone, or change it – for example – to run weekly as I have in Figure 16. Unless you're a computer geek, keep the check boxes checked for **Check for updated definitions before scanning** and **Apply default actions to items selected during the scan**.

If I scroll down the *Options* screen (Figure 17) you can see additional checkboxes for real-time protection. Unlike scanning, which you must run manually or set to run on a schedule, the real-time protection automatically monitors potentially harmful activities on your computer; activities like programs being set to auto-start when your computer is rebooted, or system configuration settings being changed without your knowledge.

The recommendation is to check all of the real-time protection boxes, or leave them alone if already checked.

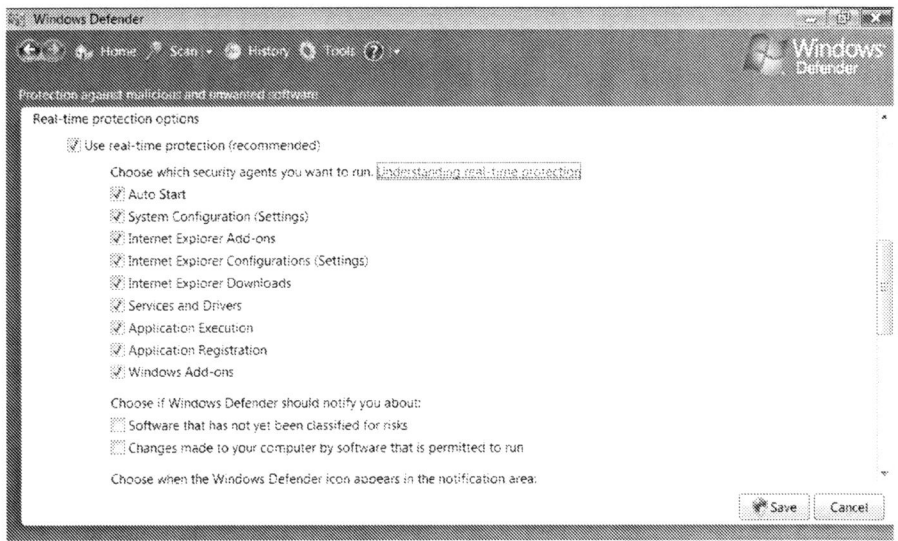

Figure 17 Windows Defender Options, real-time protection

I don't want to make this any more complicated than it needs to be, so my coverage of Windows Defender will end there. The default options should suffice for most home users, and there's plenty of help documentation on-line and within the product itself to cater for the needs of more advanced users.

Other security settings

I've taken you through the three main components of Windows Security Center: firewall, automatic updating, and malware protection.

By scrolling down the Windows Security Center page I can reveal a fourth category, named *Other security settings*, shown in Figure 18.

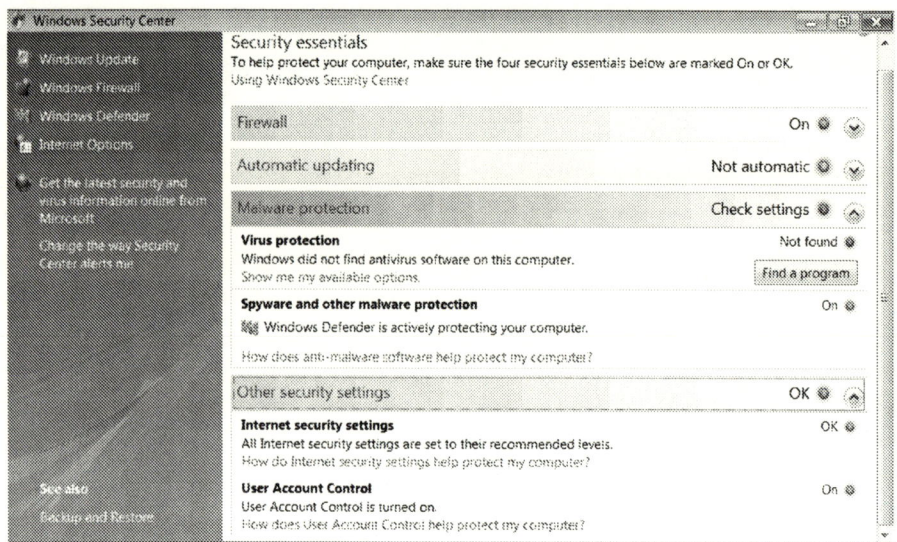

Figure 18 Windows Security Center, Other security settings

The two settings shown – *Internet security settings* and *User Account Control* – are shown as **OK** and **On** for me. The first setting should be OK by default for you too, but the second setting will almost certainly be **Off** because you've not yet followed the instructions described in the next chapter *2 – User Accounts*.

Computers Running Windows XP

If you have computers in your household running the older Windows XP, you'll be pleased to hear that you can apply the same protection on those computers. The original version of Windows XP does not include Security Center but you can get this as part of the free Windows XP Service Pack 2 (SP2) from www.microsoft.com/windowsxp/sp2/default.mspx.

Once you've downloaded SP2 and installed it on your Windows XP computer(s) you can go on to download and install Windows Defender from www.microsoft.com/athome/security/spyware/software/default.mspx.

Once you've brought your additional Windows XP computer(s) up-to-date with SP2 and Windows Defender, you can return to the beginning of this chapter and follow the steps to ensure your security settings are correct.

Summary

By following the instructions in this chapter you will have checked the security settings of the computer itself and its Windows Vista or XP operating system.

In the next chapter you will set up a user account for each person who will use the computer.

2 – User Accounts

Objective: To create appropriate user accounts on the single family computer or on individual users' computers.

You've set up your computer, secured it using Windows Security Center, and have a single account to log on with. Now you need to set up user accounts for each of the family members who will use the computer.

To start with, I'll assume you have a single family computer. Then, I'll explore the alternative of each family member having their own computer.

Accessing User Accounts

Press the Windows **Start** button and select **Control Panel** from the pop-up menu.

If you're in the *Control Panel Home* view, switch to *Classic View* by clicking the **Classic View** text. Then select the **User Accounts** item as shown in Figure 19.

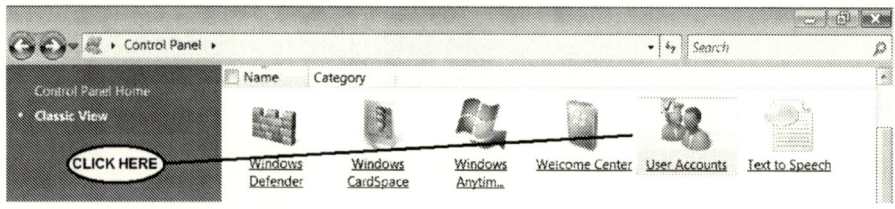

Figure 19 Control Panel, Classic View

The *User Accounts* page will be displayed (Figure 20), allowing you to perform a range of functions – on your own user account plus other user accounts that we will create shortly. In Figure 20 that follows, you can see that the **Create a password for your account** link is available to me. That's because the default administrator account on this computer, which has full administrator privileges, has not yet been secured with a password.

If that's the case for you too, click that link now to set a password; so that only you can administer the computer.

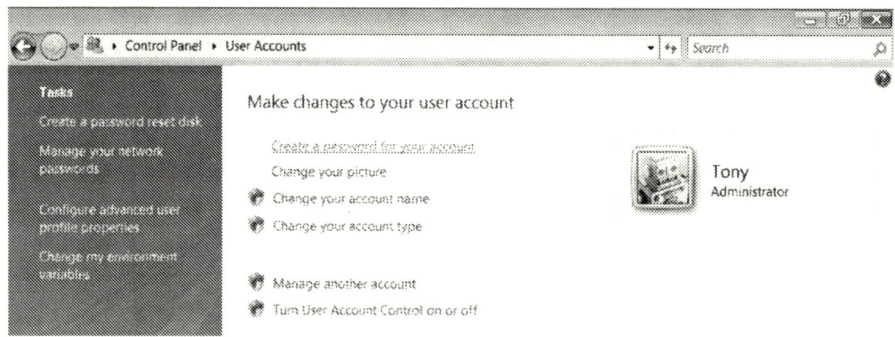

Figure 20 User Accounts page

You will have given the default account a name when you set up the computer, and you can change that name by selecting the **Change your account name** link. Using your own name is best, but you could alternatively use a generic name like *Parental Admin* if you prefer.

Adding more User Accounts

You should always add additional user accounts, one per family member, rather than allowing everyone to access the computer through the default administration account. Not only does this allow you to set different levels of access for each user, but also it allows each user's data – documents, figures etc. – to be kept separate from each other.

Clicking the **Manage another account** link on the *User Accounts* page (Figure 16) will take you to the following *Manage Accounts* page.

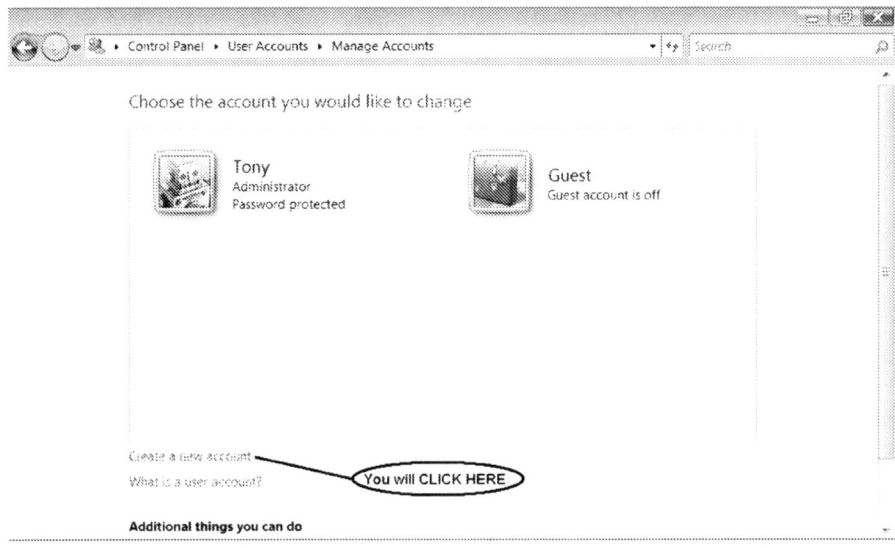

Figure 21 Manage Accounts page

In Figure 21 you can see my default, password protected, administrator account named *Tony*; plus an additional *Guest* user account which is currently switched off. We'll leave the Guest account switched off as that account allows anyone to use the computer, albeit with much-reduced privileges.

What I want to do is create user accounts for each of my family members, which I'll do by selecting the **Create a new account** link. The *Create New Account* page (shown in

Figure 22) allows me to enter a name for the user, and set their account type as **Standard user** or **Administrator**.

I name the new account *Rebecca* (let's assume it's my daughter) and set her account type to *Standard user*.

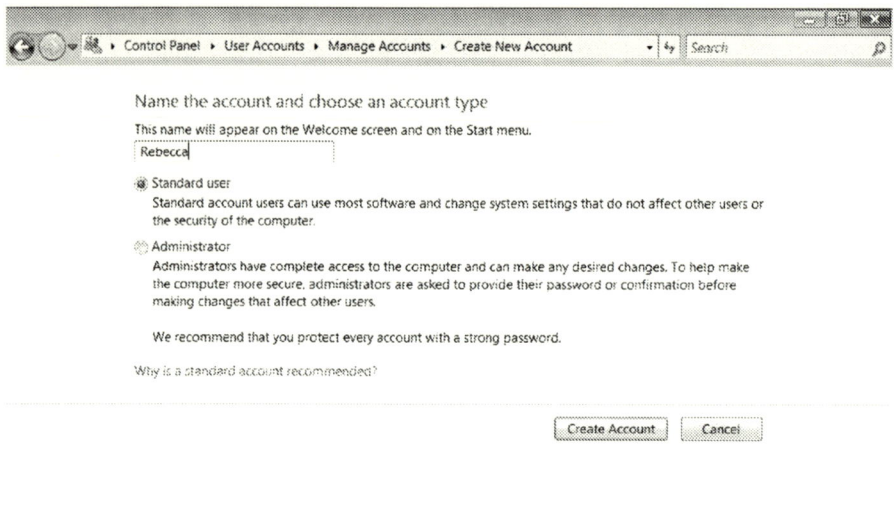

Figure 22 Create New Account page

I then repeat those steps to set up an account for *Matthew (Standard user)*, my son, and *Debbie (Administrator)*, my wife.

The end result is as follows.

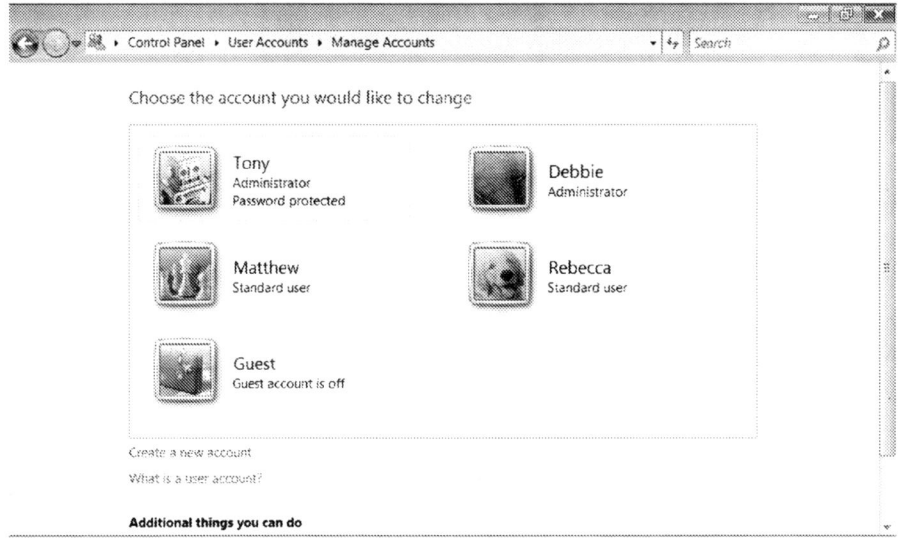

Figure 23 Manage Accounts page showing new user accounts

Logging on to User Accounts

Each time the computer is started, the set of user accounts from which the user can choose will be displayed. If the selected account has a password, you will be prompted to enter it.

Every family member should always use their own user account.

You can also switch to another user account temporarily, without logging off the current account or restarting the computer, by selecting the **Switch User** as shown next.

Figure 24 Switch User

The *Switch User* option was accessed by clicking the Windows **Start** button followed by the **right-pointing arrow** to the right of the padlock symbol. You are presented with a list of user accounts from which to choose.

User Files

As each user logs in for the first time a portion of the computer's file system is allocated for that user's files. A simplified view of the file system structure is as follows.


```
Vista OS (C:)
→ Users
        → Tony
        → Debbie
        → Matthew
        → Rebecca
```

What this means is that all of my files will be stored by default in file location C:\Users\Tony (a folder named 'Tony' within a folder named 'Users' on the C drive).

In reality you don't need to worry too much about the file location because, as you save and load files, you will be taken to your user area automatically. For example: if Matthew uses the Paint program to create a picture, he will be prompted to save it in folder *Matthew → Pictures* as you can see in Figure 25.

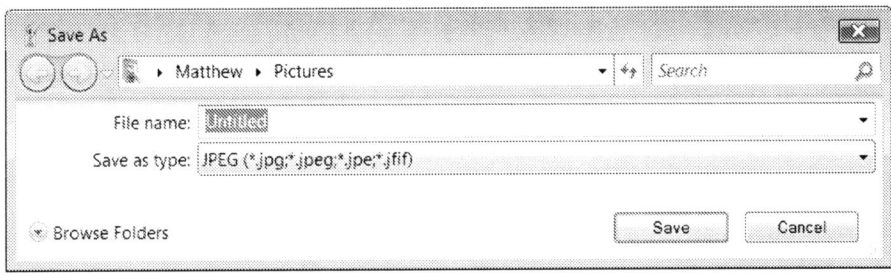

Figure 25 Save As dialog

Each user's files are secured from access from other users; i.e. they're private. If Matthew tried to access files in Rebecca's user area, he would be denied and prompted to ask for an administrator – Tony or Debbie – to grant the access.

One consequence of this is that administrator user accounts have access to all users' files on that computer – including other administrators. As you can see in Figure 26, I (Tony, an administrator) can access the folders within the user area for Debbie (the other administrator).

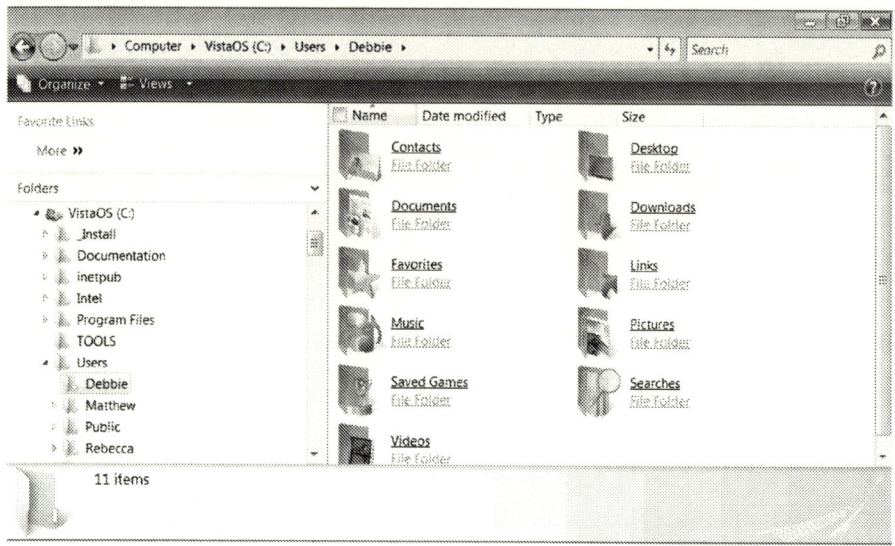

Figure 26 User folders

There is no obvious way around this, so multiple administrators on a single family computer must trust each other. Where each family member has their own computer, we can do something about it.

A Computer for each Family Member

If each family member has their own computer rather than a single one shared between them, you can organize the user accounts as follows.

- On each of the children's computers have at least one 'administrator' account in the name of a parent and a 'standard user' account for the child.

- On each of the adult's computers have an 'administrator' account only for the adult user of that computer.

That's the minimum configuration to allow each child access to their computer, to provide parental control of each child's computer, and to assure privacy between parents.

In reality in our household we have a user account for every family member on every computer, with child accounts always set as type 'standard user', and with adult accounts set as type 'standard user' on the other adult's computer but set as 'administrator' on their own computer. This means that, in the event of a computer breakdown, any family member can use any computer. Each user has a private area on every computer; private, that is, from everyone except the computer's administrator. Spouses, beware!

Note that although each user has access to a computer in the event of a breakdown, that doesn't mean they have access to their files. Backup your files regularly, so that you can copy them to your user area on another computer if you need to.

Remote Access to User Accounts

While setting up home networking is beyond the scope of this book, it is worth noting that a user account on a computer can also be used for remote access (over the home network) to that computer.

If ever you try to gain access to another computer on the network, and it asks you for a username and password, the username and password for your account on that computer should do the trick; at least as far as giving you access to your files on that computer.

Computers running Windows XP

Actually, some of the computers in our household run the older Windows XP operating system rather than the newer Windows Vista.

Although the user interface is slightly different, individual user accounts for family members can be set up in pretty much the same way. Open the Windows XP *Control Panel* and choose the **User Accounts** item.

Summary

By following the instructions in this chapter you will have created appropriate user accounts on the single family computer or on individual users' computers.

In the next chapter we'll look at how you can provide a safer web browsing experience by using web restrictions.

3 – Parental Controls, Web Restrictions

Objective: To set web restrictions on user accounts.

Of greatest concern to parents and other responsible adults will be their childrens' access to the World Wide Web. Windows Vista Parental Controls (Web Restrictions) allows you to restrict access to web sites on a per-user basis, either explicitly (by constructing a list) or implicitly (via automatic content filters), so that family members are not exposed to inappropriate content.

Accessing Parental Controls

You can access parental controls from *Control Panel* in either *Control Panel Home* or *Classic View* mode as shown in Figure 27 and Figure 28 below.

Figure 27 Control Panel Home

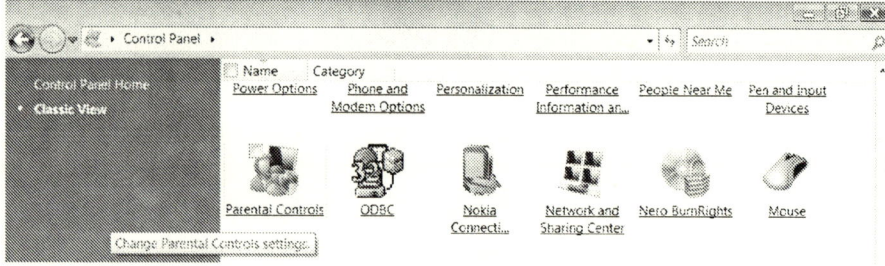

Figure 28 Control Panel, Classic View

Upon entering **Parental Controls** for the first time you might be warned that one or more administrator accounts do not have a password, as I have been warned in Figure 29.

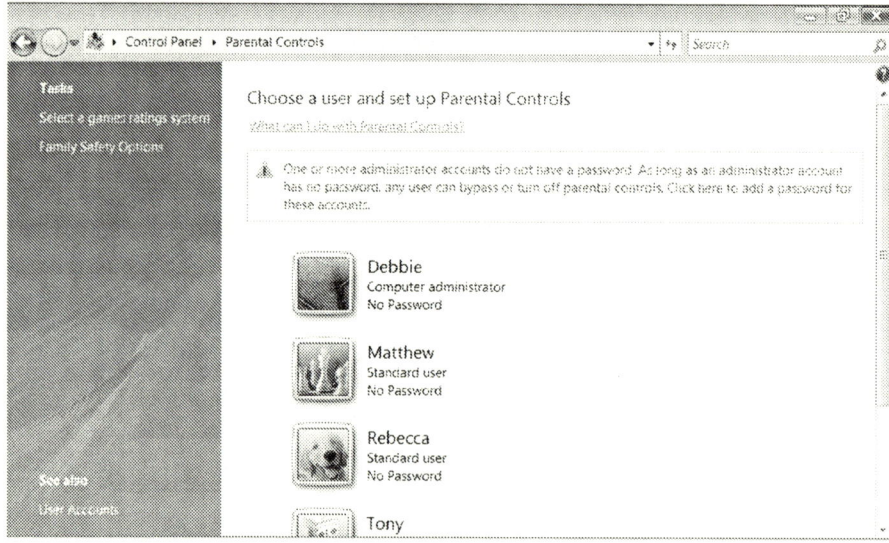

Figure 29 Parental Controls page

That's because I did not set an initial password at the time that I set up an administrator account for my wife, Debbie.

Without a password on every administrator account, parental controls could be circumvented by the (child) user simply selecting that administrator user account from the log-on screen. If you're in the same position as me, don't worry as you'll be prompted to put that right by entering a password at the next step. I strongly recommend that you do so.

To access the parental control settings for a particular user you simply select that user from the displayed list; but note that you cannot set parental controls for an administrator user.

Selecting **Matthew** takes me to the following page:

Figure 30 User Controls page

Initially *Parental Controls* will be set to **Off**.

You can see above that I have clicked the radio button marked **On, enforce current settings**.

Web Restrictions

On the right of the Figure 30 you can see that *Web Restrictions* for Matthew are currently set to **Medium**. I click the link labeled **Medium** so that I can change Matthew's settings via the page shown next.

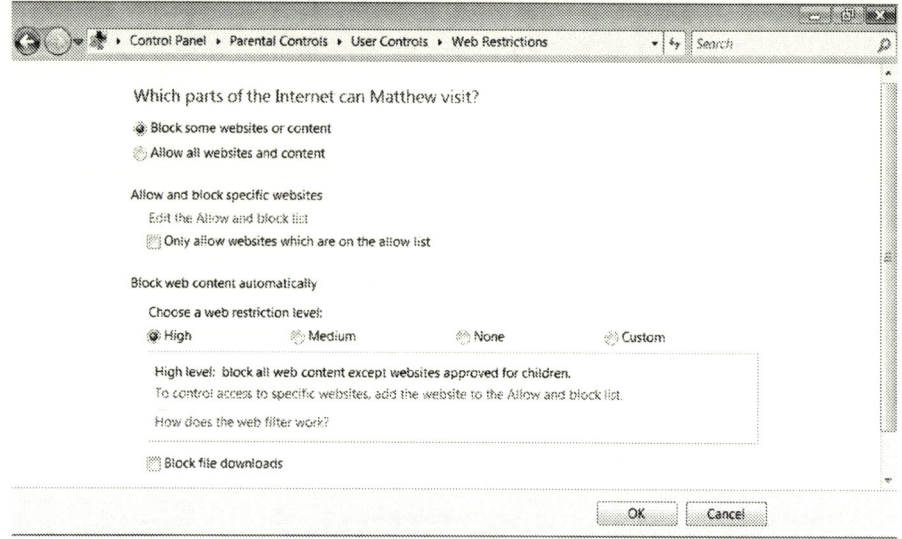

Figure 31 Web Restrictions page

Block some websites or content should already be selected, and the *web restriction level* – initially set to **Medium** – can be set to a higher or lower level as appropriate. I have changed the *web restriction level* to **High**.

The four levels are:

High – block all web content except web sites approved for children.

Medium – block unratable content and web content in the following categories: mature content, pornography, drugs, hate speech, and weapons. Not all content in these areas can be automatically blocked.

None – no web content is automatically blocked.

Custom – select the content categories that you want to block.

The final **Custom** setting deserves a figure (Figure 32) to show you which content categories you can block, albeit not guaranteed.

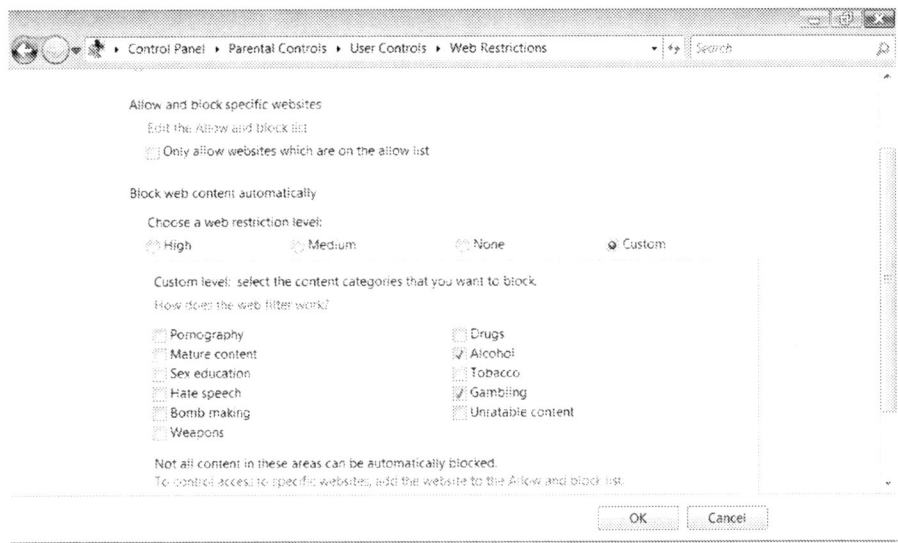

Figure 32 Web Restrictions page, Custom web restriction level

Here I've specified that I'm quite happy for Matthew to access content related to **Alcohol** or **Gambling**, but none of the other categories. Don't judge my parenting skills, it's just an example!

Testing the web restrictions

I tested the web restrictions by logging in under Matthew's user account and attempting to visit various web sites using Internet Explorer. I could access the Children's BBC web site at www.bbc.co.uk/cbbc and the Disney website at disney.go.com. I could not access...

Sorry, I can't tell you which unsavory web sites I tried to visit; nor can I tell you the name of the person who recommended them to me!

When I said that I could access the child-oriented web sites, I didn't mean that I could access them fully. In each case, a message appeared across the top of the browser page indicating:

Some content on the page has been blocked by Windows Parental Controls. Click here for options...

In the case of the CBBC web site, the majority of the content was accessible, and only a few images were not displayed on the page. These were only images such as the CBBC logo itself, so need not have been denied, but it's better to be safe than sorry I suppose.

In the case of the Disney web site, no content at all was displayed; as can be seen in Figure 33.

Figure 33 View Blocked Content prompt

Whenever content is blocked in this way it is always possible for the (child) user to select the **View Blocked Content** option, which prompts for an administrator password. The problem, though, is that one lot of blocked content often leads to another – which means repeated calls to the parent to enter the administrator password. Don't ever be tempted to give the administrator password to the child, as that completely defeats the object of having one!

Next, I adjusted Matthew's web restriction level from **High** to **Medium**, and tried again. This time I was prevented from accessing the unsavory web sites (which I'm still not telling you) and was granted unhindered access to the CBBC and Disney web sites. For the record, I was also granted access to the BBC news web site at news.bbc.co.uk including stories relating to pedophiles and child prostitution. That's no worse than the news stories that might be broadcast on television during my children's viewing hours.

So it seems to me that the **Medium** setting strikes the right balance between what my children can access, and the number of times I wish to be called to enter a password. Having used other parental control systems such as Yahoo! Parental Controls, I know how onerous that can be.

Of course, the **High** setting might be more appropriate for very young children... and grannies!

Allow and block list
Although the automatic content filtering works well enough, it is not guaranteed to filter out 100% of unsuitable content. If you find that a user has been able to access an inappropriate web site despite the automatic web restrictions, you can block that site explicitly. Conversely if you find a web site blocked which you do wish to be accessible, you can allow that site explicitly.

On the main *Web Restrictions* page (Figure 31) you can find a link labeled **Edit the Allow and block list**, which takes you to the following *Allow Block Webpages* page.

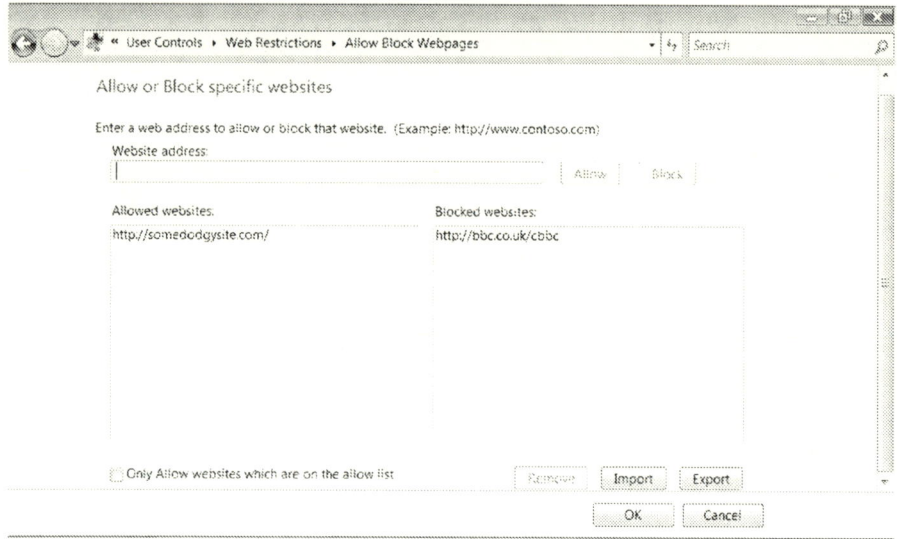

Figure 34 Allow Block Webpages page

You can type a web site address into the **Web site address** box and press the **Allow** or **Block** button to override the automatic control of that site. My entries into the *Allow websites* and *Block websites* lists mean that:

- Access to web site www.somedodgysite.com will be granted even if the automatic web restriction attempts to block it.

- Access to web site www.bbc.co.uk/cbbc will be denied even if the automatic web restriction attempts to allow it.

Whenever a user visits a new web site and is prompted for administrator authorization, that web site is added automatically to the allow list once you enter your administrator password. In that way, the allow list pretty much takes care of itself without you having to build the list yourself.

If you really want to lock down web access, you can click the checkbox labeled **Only allow websites which are on the allow list**. You can then control exactly the list of web sites that can be accessed, but be prepared for numerous requests to authorize new pages!

Block File Downloads

Also on the main *Web Restrictions* page (Figure 31) you can see a checkbox labeled **Block file downloads**. It does what it says, and prevents the user from downloading potentially harmful files to the computer's hard disk.

Two ways to test this, for your peace of mind, are as follows:

- Log in using the restricted user's account, find a link to a downloadable file and try to download it. For example, visit www.lulu.com/content/1191735, right-click the link labeled **Preview this book**, and choose **Save Target As**.

- Log in using the restricted user's account, visit a software supplier such as Adobe (at www.adobe.com) and try to download one of their free software programs.

In both cases you will be prevented by parental controls.

In the second case, this might occasionally present a small problem; the problem being that some web sites only work correctly if you download and install an add-on such as the Adobe Flash Player. In this situation you will need to temporarily disable parental controls, or temporarily allow downloads, so that you can download and install the add-on.

Only install well-known add-ons from reputable companies such as Microsoft and Adobe.

Computers Running Windows XP

If any of your computers run the older Windows XP, the bad news is that you will not be able to use parental controls on those computers, unless you sign up for the Windows Live OneCare described in Appendix A – Windows XP Family Safety. However, you can restrict Internet access on the computer as follows.

Launch Internet Explorer and choose **Internet Options** from the **Tools** menu. Then select the **Content** tab so that you see the *Content Advisor* setting as shown next in Figure 35.

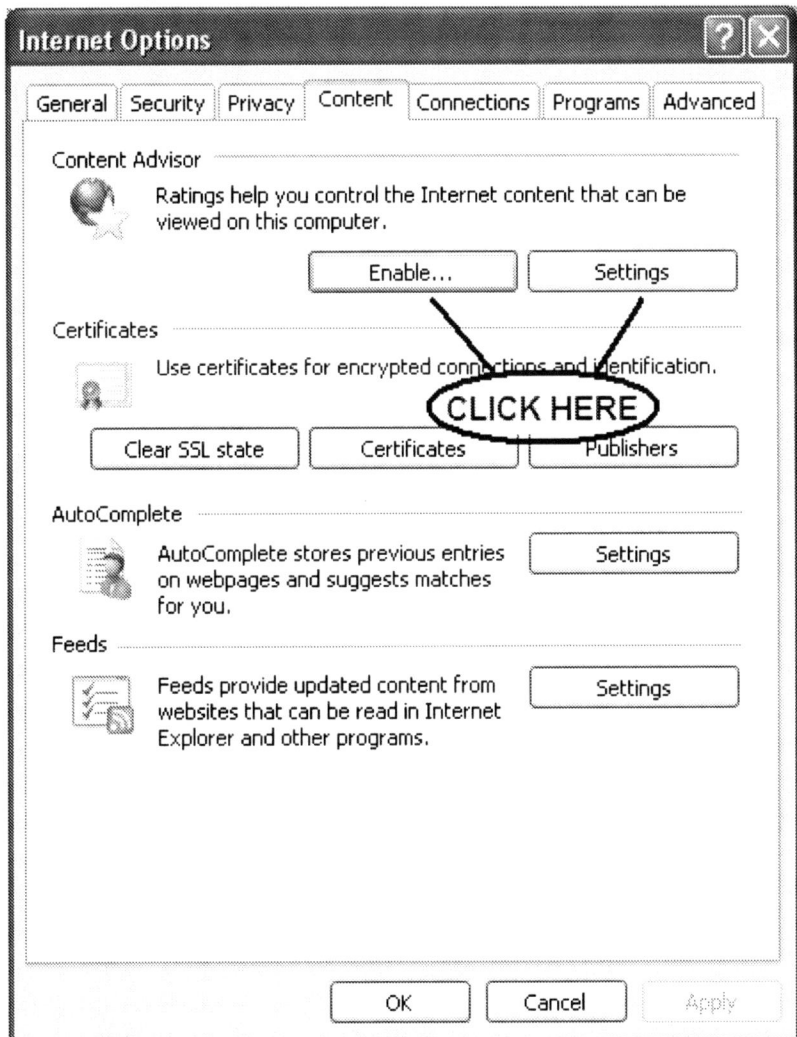

Figure 35 Internet Options, Content tab

You can click the **Enable** button to enable the Content Advisor, and by pressing the **Settings** button you can see the current Content Advisor settings.

What does Content Advisor give you? Pretty much the same as the parental control web restrictions described earlier; except that Content Advisor is a blunter instrument that applies web restrictions settings to the computer as a whole, not per user.

The *General Tab* (see Figure 36) allows you to set a Supervisor password, which you would then need to enter to make further changes and to authorize individual sites for viewing. You can also choose a ratings system (the *Ratings* tab) and build a list of approved and denied sites (the *Approved Sites* tab).

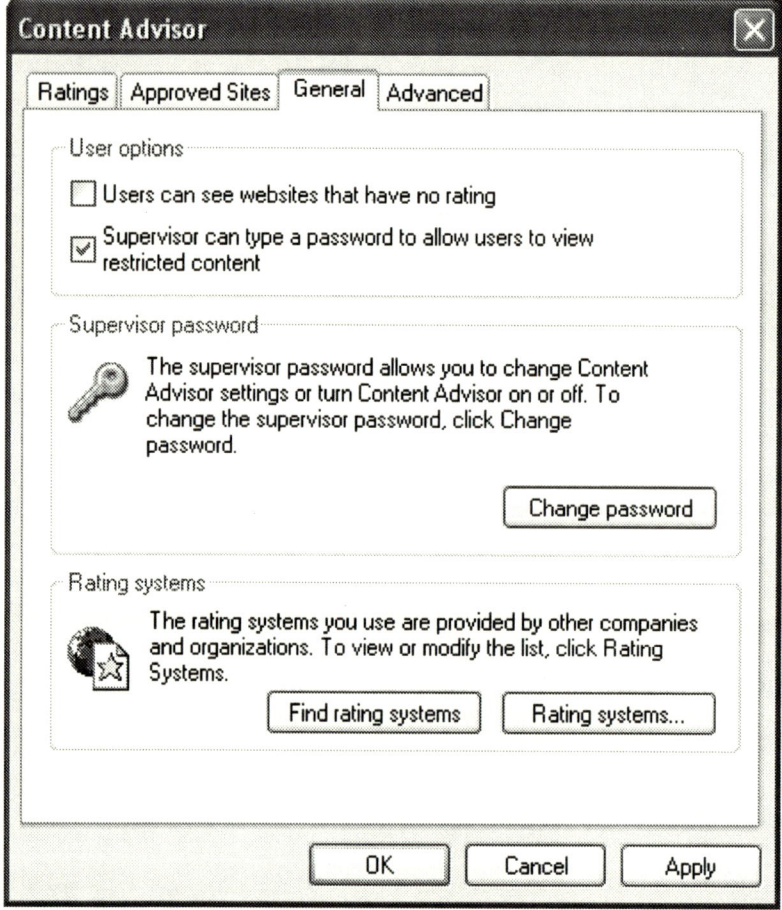

Figure 36 Content Advisor, General tab

While the specific menu options and buttons may be different, and the settings apply to the whole computer, the concepts are essentially the same as those we've covered in the first part of this chapter.

Summary

By following these instructions you will have provided a safer web browsing experience, by setting parental control web restrictions on individual user accounts.

In the next chapter we'll look at the other parental controls provided by Windows Vista.

4 – Other Parental Controls

Objective: To set other parental controls on individual user accounts.

In addition to the web restrictions covered in the previous chapter, there are additional parental controls that may be applied to user accounts.

As described previously, select the **Parental Controls** items in the *Control Panel (Classic View)* or select the **Set up parental controls for any user** link from the *User Accounts and Family Safety* section of the *Control Panel Home*. For a reminder, look back at Figure 28 and Figure 27.

The *Parental Controls* page (shown previously in Figure 29) will be displayed, and from there you can enter the *User Controls* page (shown again in Figure 37) for a particular user account – by clicking on the appropriate user account.

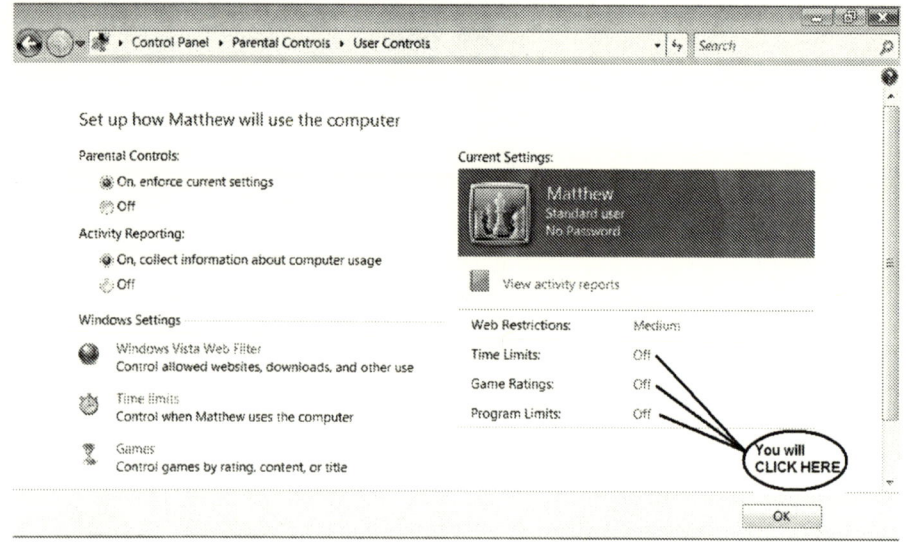

Figure 37 User Controls page

You can see that the other parental control settings are *Time Limits*, *Game Ratings* and *Program Limits*, in addition to the *Web Restrictions* covered in the previous chapter.

I'll take each one in turn, but first a note about the **Windows Vista Web Filter** link on the left of the page. This takes you nowhere new; it simply takes you to the same *Web Restrictions* page that we visited earlier.

Now we'll look at the other parental controls, starting with Time Limits.

Time Limits

You can access the Time Limits page from the *User Controls* page by clicking the **Time Limits** link (to the left of the page), or the *Time Limits* **On / Off** link (to the right of the page).

In Figure 38 you can see that I have blocked out certain times each day when I do not want Matthew to be using the computer. In a nutshell I am allowing him a maximum of two hours usage each evening, and up to nine hours per day at the weekend.

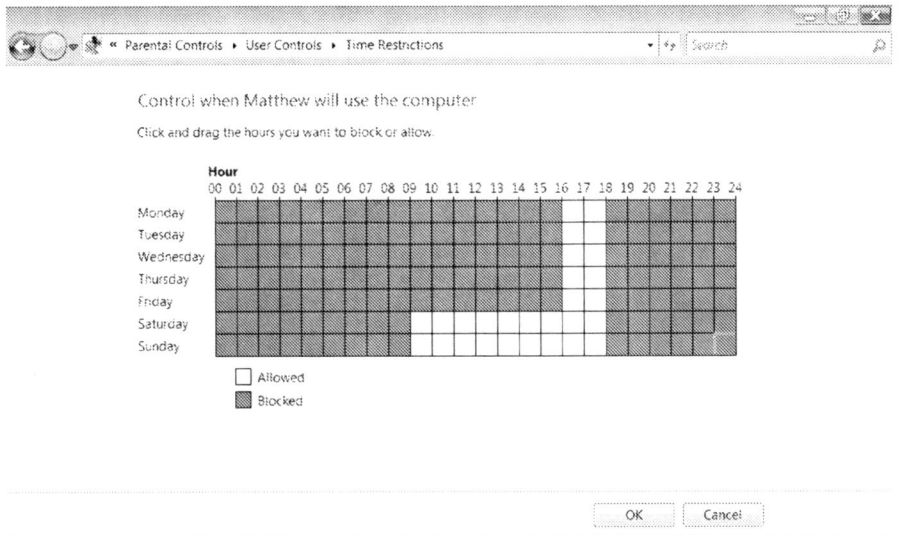

Figure 38 Time Restrictions

Blocking out time is as easy as clicking boxes to toggle them between *Allowed* and *Blocked* status, and you can even click-and-drag to block out whole areas.

When Matthew tries to log on at an unapproved time he will be rewarded with the message:

```
Logon   failure:   account   logon   time   restriction
violation
```

If a user strays in to a blocked time zone while already logged in, he or she will be logged out automatically – but not without warning. A warning message will appear on the user's screen at 15 minutes-to-go and 1-minute-to-go to say something like:

```
Windows  Parental  Controls
```

```
You will be logged out in 1 minute.
```

According to Microsoft's on-line documentation:

"If their time ends before they log off the computer, Windows Vista suspends their session and displays the logon screen so another user can use the computer. The child's session stays active in the background, however, so the next time they log on, they can pick up where they left off without losing any of their work."

Game Ratings

There have been several examples over the years of video games that have courted controversy; including Mortal Kombat (violence), Grand Theft Auto (crime) and Duke Nukem 3D (sex).

The *Game Controls* page shown in Figure 39 is accessible via the **Games** link or the *Game Rating* **On** / **Off** link on the *User Controls* page (Figure 37).

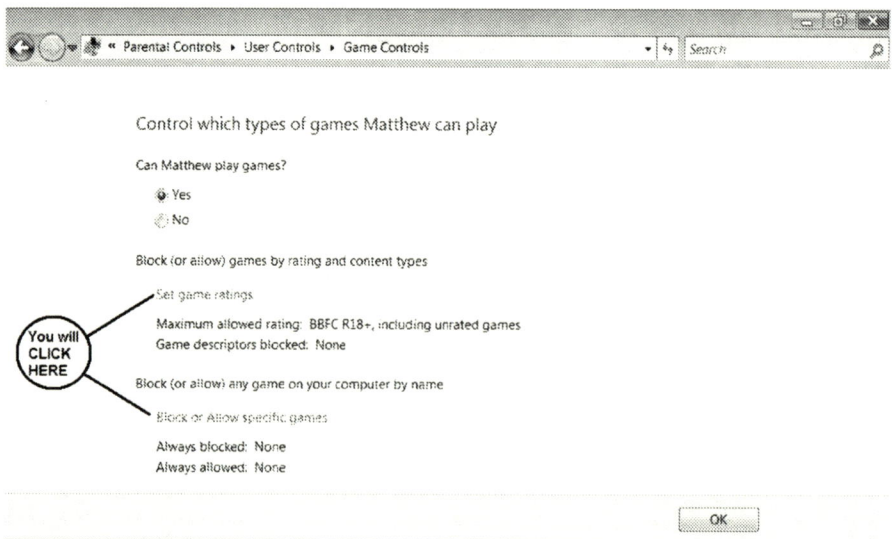

Figure 39 Game Controls page

This page allows you to specify whether or not the user can play games at all, allows you to **Set game ratings**, and allows you to **Block or Allow specific games**.

Set game ratings

By selecting the **Set game ratings** link on the *Game Controls* page you can access the *Game Restrictions* page (shown next in Figure 40).

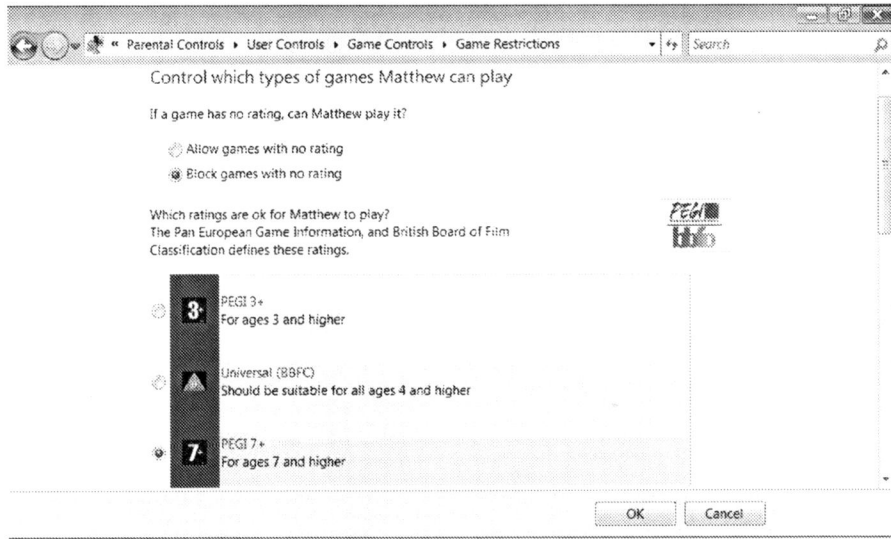

Figure 40 Game Restrictions page, upper portion

This page allows you to determine whether unrated games should be automatically allowed or blocked, and lets you choose a rating level for allowable games.

I have opted to **Block games with no rating** (the safest option), and allow games rated by the Pan European Game Information (PEGI) as suitable for ages 7 and higher.

The game ratings schemes available to you may differ depending on your jurisdiction. Since I am located in the UK

I can choose from the rating schemes of PEGI and the British Board of Film Classification (BBFC). Those of you located in the United States should be able to choose from ratings provided by the Entertainment Software Ratings Board (ESRB).

By scrolling down the *Game Restrictions* page (Figure 41) I can reveal additional check boxes, which provide finer-grained control for blocking games based on their content.

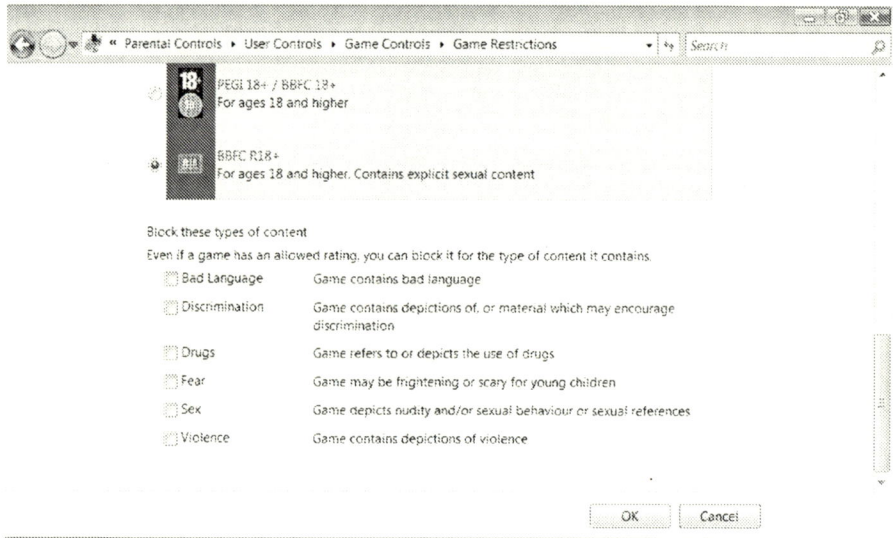

Figure 41 Game Restrictions page, lower portion

For example: even if a game has a suitable age rating, I might want to block it if it contains any sexual behavior or sexual references. After all, I might be setting the game restrictions for my granny; and she's ok with violence but not with sex.

Block or Allow Specific Games

Do you remember that web restrictions allowed you to build up lists of explicitly-allowed and explicitly-blocked web sites that took precedence over the automatic settings? Well, it's the same with games.

If I know a particular game well, I might decide that I don't want my children to play it despite the favorable rating. For another game, I might decide that my children <u>can</u> play it despite its <u>unfavorable</u> rating.

Merely for illustration, in Figure 42 (next) I have selectively allowed and disallowed some of the pre-installed Windows games. And in case you haven't figured it out, I got to this *Game Overrides* page by clicking the **Block or Allow specific games** link on the *Game Controls* page (Figure 39, shown previously).

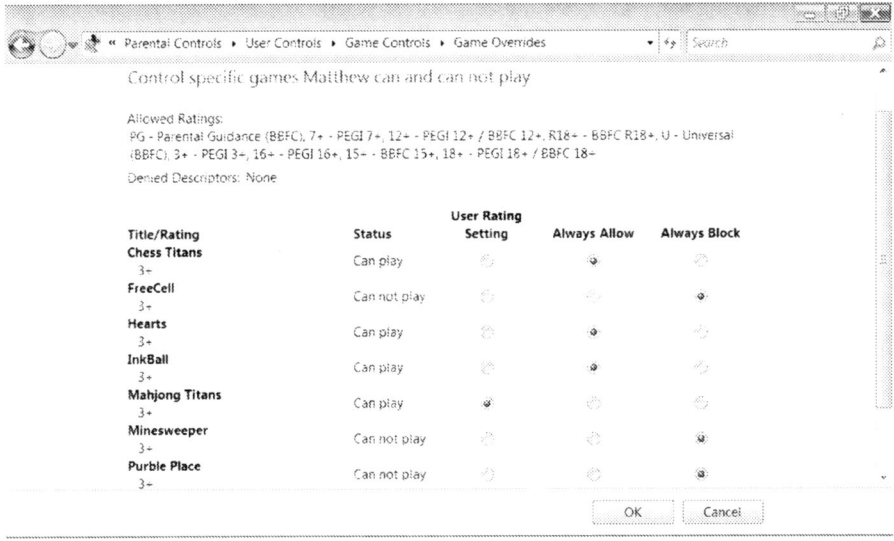

Figure 42 Game Overrides

Having made those changes, and pressed **OK**, I can then see the lists of blocked and allowed games at the bottom of the *Game Controls* page (Figure 43).

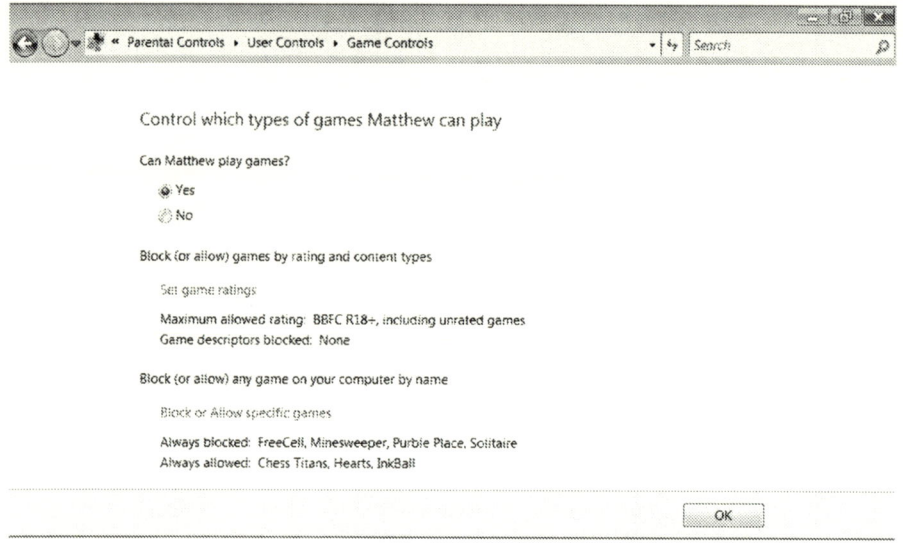

Figure 43 Game Controls page, blocked and allowed games

Program Limits

Games represent entertainment products that can be rated in the same way that videos and DVDs can be rated.

Typically there will be other non-entertainment programs installed on the family computer, which you might not want certain users to run. For example: I might be happy for my daughter to create documents using Microsoft Word, but not to use my hard disk recover utility.

So I go to the *User Controls* page for my daughter (by now you know how) and there I click the *Program Limits* **On** / **Off** link. Look back at Figure 37 if you need a reminder.

The *Application Restrictions* page is displayed, as shown in Figure 44, and is populated with the programs currently installed on the computer.

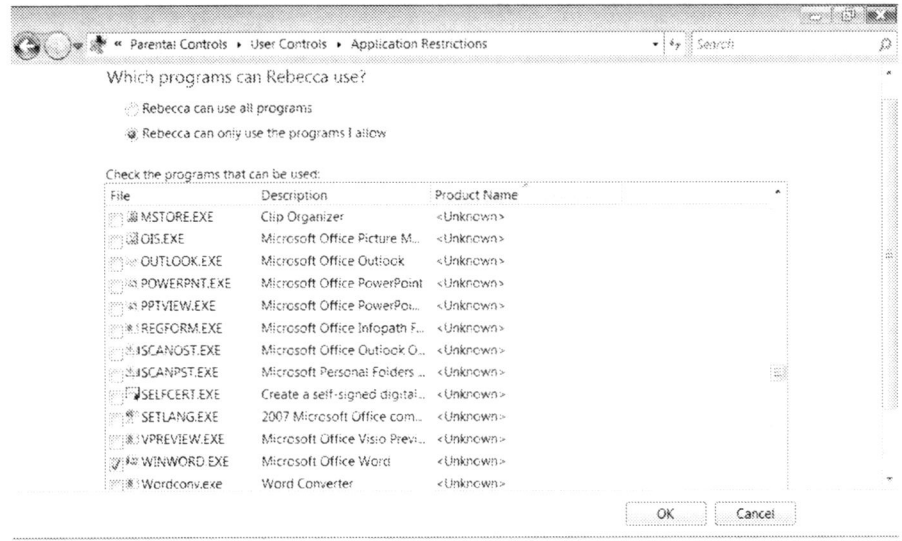

Figure 44 Application Restrictions

I want Rebecca to use only Microsoft Word, remember, so I check the box next to *WINWORD.EXE Microsoft Office Word*.

I then test the settings by logging on as Rebecca, attempting to launch Microsoft Word, and then attempting to launch other programs.

Summary

By following the instructions in this chapter you will have set other parental controls -- Time Limits, Game Ratings, and Program Limits – on individual user accounts.

In the next chapter we'll look at how you can monitor the computing activities of family members by using activity reports.

5 – Activity Reports

Objective: To monitor family members' computing activities using activity reports.

Do you remember that web restrictions did not guarantee that all undesirable content could be blocked automatically? Even if you can't block it, you can at least detect it. And if you can detect it, you can block it manually.

Welcome to Activity Reports.

Enabling Activity Reporting

You enable activity reporting on a per-user basis, from the specific user's *Parental Controls*, *User Controls* page. Figure 45 shows the User Controls page for Matthew, on which you can see an *Activity Reporting* radio button labeled **On, collect information about computer usage**. Click that radio button to switch on activity reporting for the user.

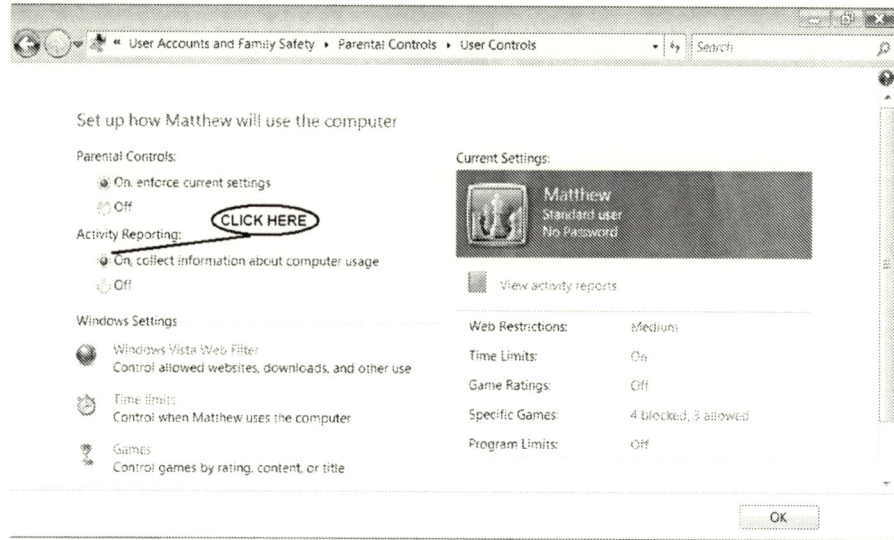

Figure 45 Parental Controls, User Controls

You can also see in Figure 45 a link labeled **View activity reports**. Clicking that link is one way to view the activity reports, not just for this user but for all the other computer users too. Another way is to select the **View activity reports** link from the *User Accounts and Family Safety* category of *Control Panel* (Figure 46).

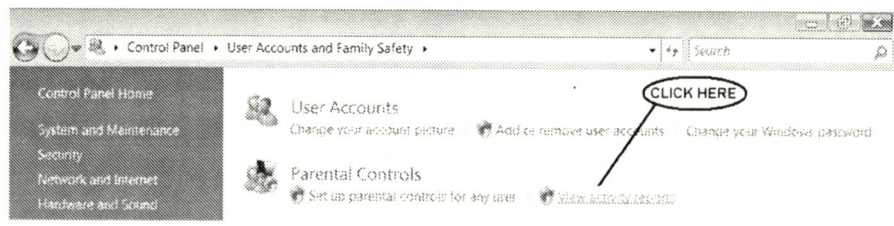

Figure 46 Control Panel, User Accounts and Family Safety

Viewing activity reports

The *Activity Viewer* page (Figure 47) lists the individual user names down the left-hand side. When you click on one of those names you see a summary report for that user in the main panel to the right.

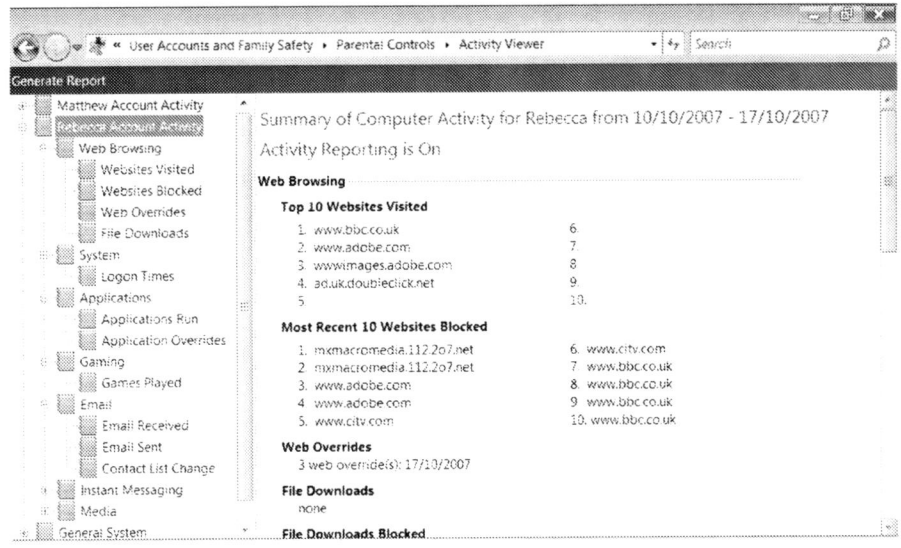

Figure 47 Activity Viewer, #1

The first part of the activity summary report shows the web sites that have been visited regularly, those that have been blocked, and the number of blocks that have been overridden (by you entering an administrator password). You can also see (at the bottom) that file downloads and blocked file downloads are also listed.

The initial portion of the summary report tells you where the (child) user's activity has been concentrated, and gives you the opportunity to identify web sites that have been blocked but which you could add to the allowed list (see *3 – Parental Controls, Web Restrictions*) if you consider them to be safe.

If I scroll down the summary page to give Figure 48, you can see some of the other activity information that is available to you. Namely *Logon Times* and *Applications*:

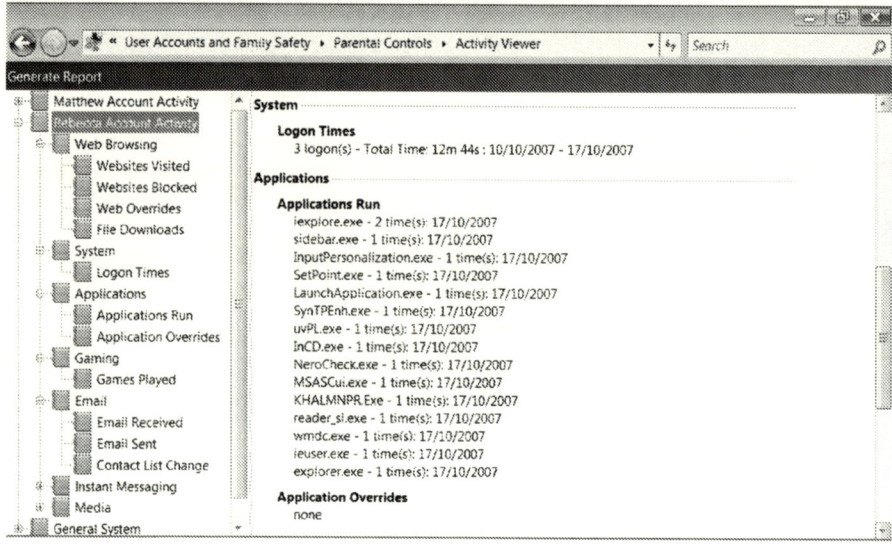

Figure 48 Activity Viewer, #2

This tells you how many times the user has logged on, and for how much time overall. It also shows you which applications the user has run, or which have been run by Windows itself on the user's behalf.

If I scroll down yet further to give Figure 49 you can see details of the user's game playing activity, e-mail usage (next chapter), instant messaging activity (using Windows Live Messenger), and media viewing (using Windows Media Player).

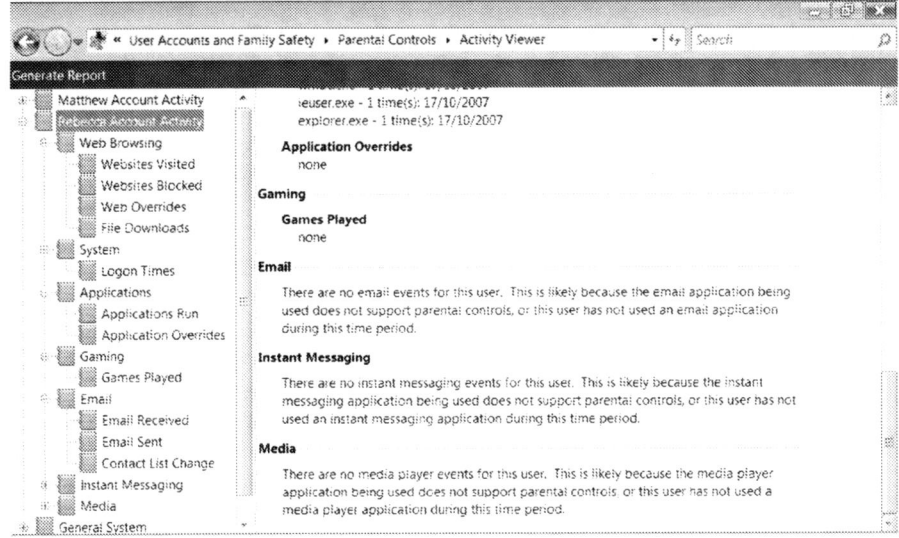

Figure 49 Activity Viewer, #3

You will notice in those figures that I have also expanded the subcategories below the user name, any one of which I can click for more detailed information.

Remember we saw a summary of *Logon Times*, which simply counted the number of logons and totaled the logon time? Well I can get more information by clicking the **Logon Times** category in the tree view like this:

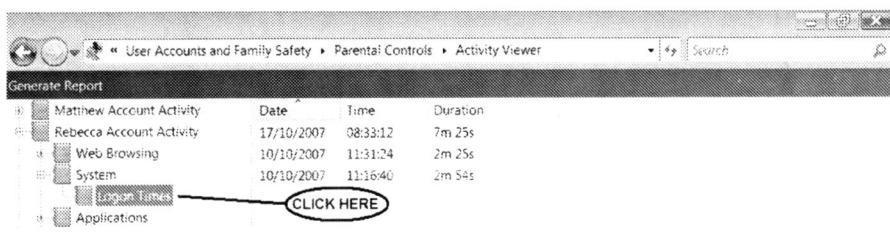

Figure 50 Activity Reports, Logon Times

Now I know exactly when the user (Rebecca) was logged on, at what time, and for how long.

Computers Running Windows XP

Unfortunately the Windows XP operating system does not include any direct equivalent to the Vista activity reports. Once again you have the option of signing up for the Windows Live OneCare described in Appendix A – Windows XP Family Safety.

Summary

By following the steps in this chapter you will have discovered a way to monitor the computing activities of family members.

In the next chapter we'll look at how Windows Vista can provide a safer e-mail environment for family members.

6 – Windows Mail

Objective: To protect e-mail users from malicious messages.

In Chapter 3 we looked at how to use web restrictions to limit your child's – or granny's – exposure to potentially harmful and morally questionable content. The World Wide Web is one possible channel for such content, but not the only one; the other obvious channel being e-mail.

If you've used e-mail for as long as I have, and – in the early days of the Internet explosion – broadcast your e-mail address in a naïve attempt to drum up business, you will now, like me, be crushed under a mountain of SPAM.

As defined at
http://spam.abuse.net/overview/whatisspam.shtml…

"Spam is flooding the Internet with many copies of the same message, in an attempt to force the message on people who would not otherwise choose to receive it. Most spam is commercial advertising, often for dubious products, get-rich-quick scams, or quasi-legal services."

I receive more non-genuine e-mail each day than genuine e-mail: everything from biologically implausible anatomical enhancements to money-for-nothing financial schemes. Not to mention invitations to 'update my on-line banking security details' (not really from my bank) and free attached software (that will likely corrupt my Windows installation).

As a result I have to take measures to avoid, eliminate, or at least redirect unwanted messages before they reach my inbox. So will you; if not now, then eventually. And of course, this issue becomes all the more important when we consider the e-mail usage of minors.

I use Windows Mail in this chapter as the vehicle for demonstrating the various e-mail protection features, because Windows Mail is the e-mail client program that comes bundled with Windows Vista. As indicated later, some of these techniques can also be applied to Outlook Express (which came bundled with the older Windows XP) and to Microsoft Office Outlook (which comes as part of the Microsoft Office suite).

Note that the steps outlined must be applied on each user account separately. So in our family I would need to log on as myself and follow these steps, log on as Matthew and follow these steps, and so on.

Windows Mail

You can launch Windows Mail by clicking the Windows **Start** menu, followed by **All Programs**, followed by **Windows Mail**; as shown in Figure 51.

Figure 51 Start, All Programs, Windows Mail

Accounts

When you signed up with your Internet Service Provider (ISP), the chances are that they provided you with one or more family e-mail addresses and details of how to use them. Alternatively, you might have signed up for an e-mail account separately with a popular provider such as Yahoo! or Google.

If you're currently using web-based e-mail with one of the popular providers you could continue to do that. Check out the facilities they provide for SPAM (junk e-mail) protection, message filtering / redirection, and disposable e-mail addresses.

Whether or not you're using web-based e-mail, your e-mail provider should have provided you with some e-mail account details that you can use to send / receive e-mail directly from your computer's e-mail program, in this case Windows Mail. You can set up an e-mail account in Windows Mail to send and receive messages as follows.

Choose **Tools** from the Windows Mail menu, and then select **Accounts**. On the *Internet Accounts* dialog (shown in Figure 52) click the **Add...** button.

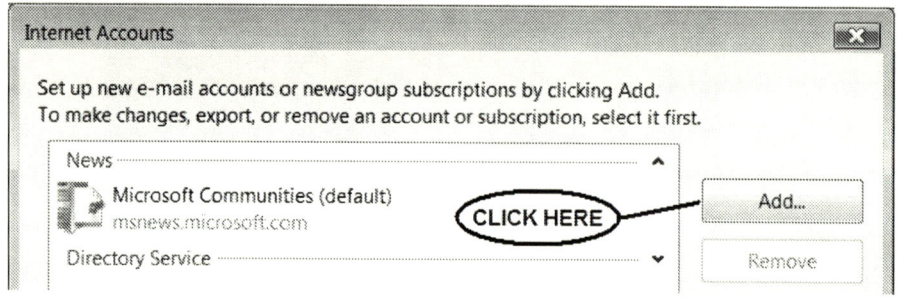

Figure 52 Internet Accounts

You will be prompted to select an account type, and you should choose **E-mail Account**. When prompted for *Your Name*, enter your name (e.g. Tony Loton); and when prompted for *Internet E-mail Address*, enter the e-mail address given to you by your e-mail provider (e.g. tony@loton.net).

The next dialog, shown in Figure 53, will ask for the details of your e-mail provider's servers (their computers). For

Incoming e-mail server type you would usually select **POP3**, but it might be **IMAP** – so check with your e-mail provider.

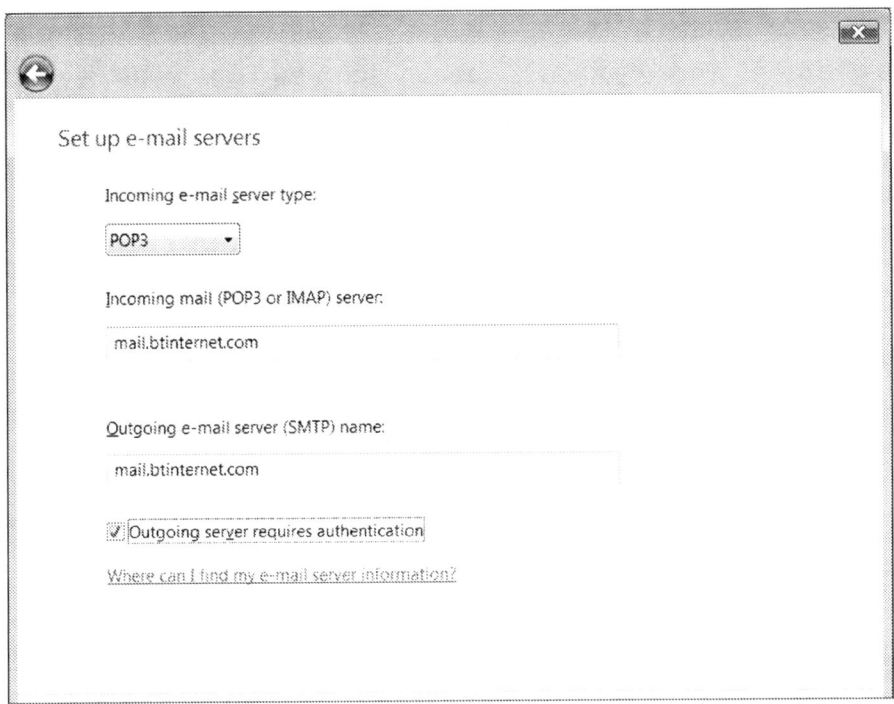

Figure 53 Set up e-mail servers

The *Incoming mail (POP3 or IMAP) server* is the e-mail provider's computer that holds your incoming messages. It might be something like **pop.yourprovider.com**, or in my case **mail.btinternet.com**.

The *Outgoing e-mail server (SMTP) name* is the name of the e-mail provider's computer that sends your outgoing messages. It might be something like **smtp.yourprovider.com**, or in my case it's once again **mail.btinternet.com**.

Your e-mail provider will tell you whether or not you should check the *Outgoing server requires authentication* checkbox. My provider used to not require that, but now it does. You will do no harm by trying it one way and, if you have problems sending messages, trying it the other way.

The next dialog in this sequence will ask you for the *E-mail username* and *Password* given to you by your e-mail provider. The username may or may not be the same as your e-mail address, and this information must be correct in order to receive incoming messages.

That's all there is to setting up an e-mail account, which you can test by sending yourself a message.

Now, the main purpose of this chapter is not to tell you how to set up an e-mail account; but to tell you how to protect the e-mail account from potentially malicious content.

The two specific features we'll look at are Junk E-mail Options and Message Rules.

Junk E-mail Options
To access this feature, choose **Junk E-mail Options** from the Windows Mail **Tools** menu like this (Figure 54):

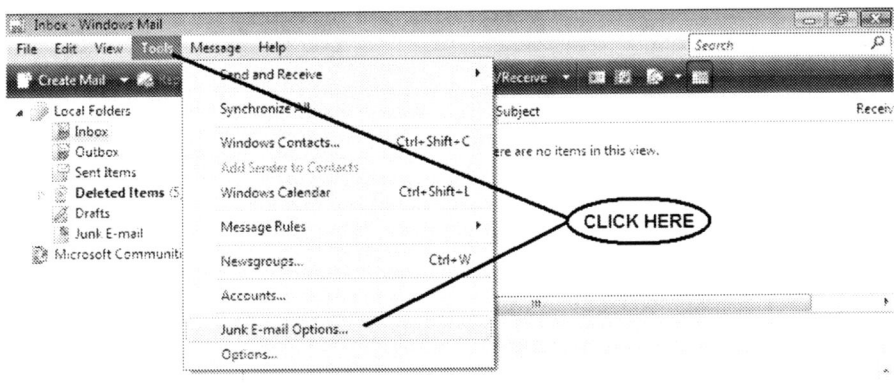

Figure 54 Tools, Junk E-mail Options

The *Junk E-mail Options* dialog will be displayed as shown in Figure 55, with the *Options* tab on display; so that you can choose a level of junk e-mail protection.

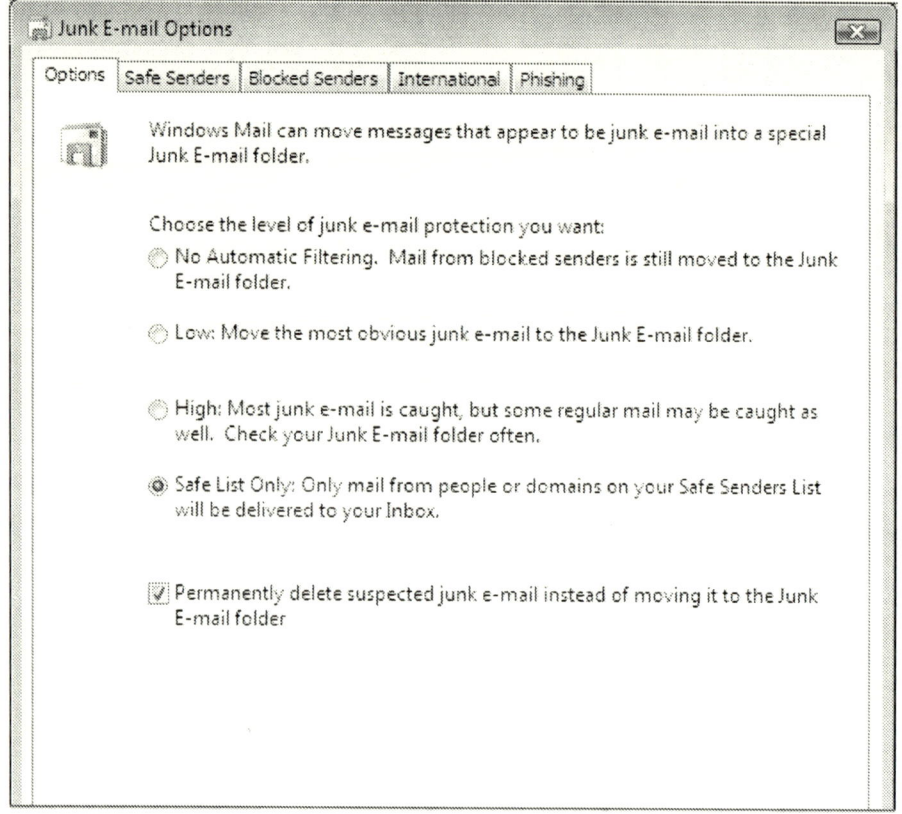

Figure 55 Junk E-mail Options, Options

When setting the options for your own account, as a parent, you might want to set this to **Low: Move the most obvious junk e-mail to the Junk E-mail folder**.

When setting the options for other family members – remember you need to log on to their user accounts – you might want to be much more cautious by choosing **Safe List Only: Only mail from people or domains on your Safe Senders List will be delivered to your Inbox**.

The point being that, for the children and grannies in your family, you will probably want to reduce the possibility of viewing offensive content down to zero; or as close as you can. To that end, in Figure 55 I have also selected the checkbox labeled **Permanently delete suspected junk e-mail instead of moving it to the Junk E-mail folder**; which means that the user will not even be aware of its existence.

If you decide to lock down e-mail access in that way, to safe senders only, you will of course have to build up a list of safe senders. You can do that in the *Safe Senders* tab as shown next in Figure 56.

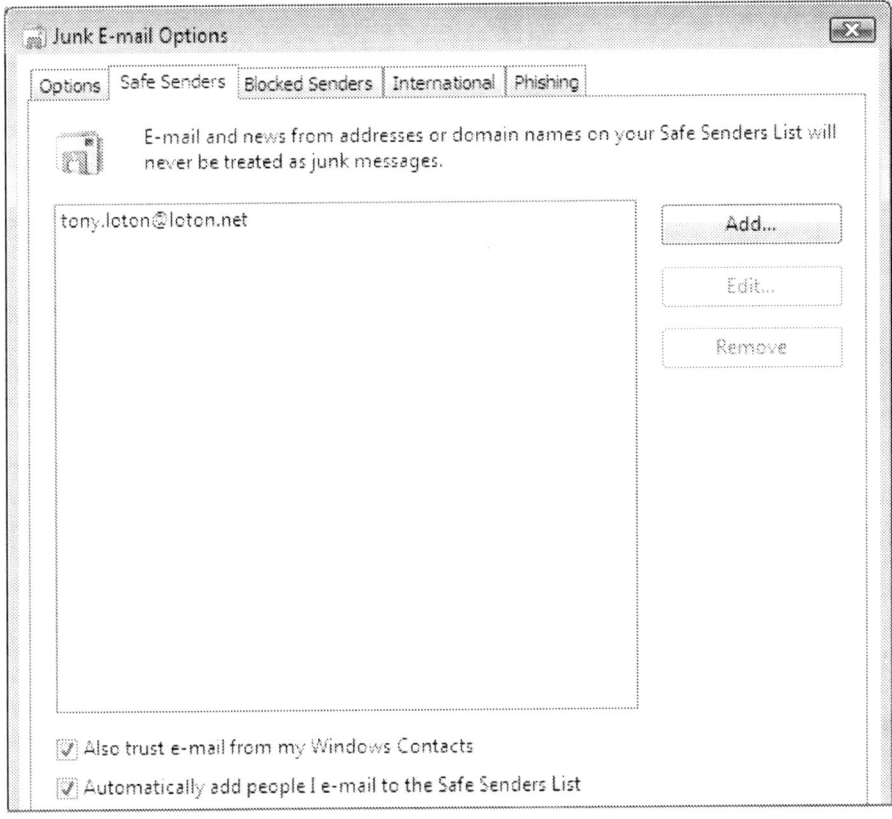

Figure 56 Junk E-mail Options, Safe Senders

Rather than explicitly having to type every single safe e-mail address into that list, I have also checked the two checkboxes:

Also trust e-mail from my Windows Contacts

and

Automatically add people I e-mail to the Safe Senders List

The second checkbox should be self-explanatory: anyone I have e-mailed is presumably someone I consider to be safe. The first checkbox raises the question "What is Windows Contacts?"

*Windows Contacts is an electronic address book that comes bundled with Windows Vista and which complements Windows Mail. You can launch it by selecting the **Windows Contacts** item from the **All Programs** category of the Windows **Start** menu.*

Looking back at the Junk E-mail Options dialog Figure 56, you will see that there are three additional tabs: *Blocked Senders*, *International*, and *Phishing*.

The *Blocked Senders* tab allows you to define a list of e-mail addresses to block even if the automatic junk e-mail handling is set to a low setting. In my case, although I'd like most e-mail to get through to me unhindered, there may be some particularly problematic senders that I would like to block.

The *International* tab allows you to block messages that originate in a particular country, such as e-mail from addresses ending *.ca* (rather than .com or .co.uk) and therefore originating in Canada. I have nothing against Canadians, it's just an example!

The *Phishing* tab allows you to block messages that Windows Mail identifies as pretending to be, for example, from your bank; but which in reality may be illegal attempts to get you to disclose personal security information.

Once you have set up the Junk E-mail Options, whenever Windows Mail detects a suspicious message you will see the following *Windows Mail* dialog (Figure 57).

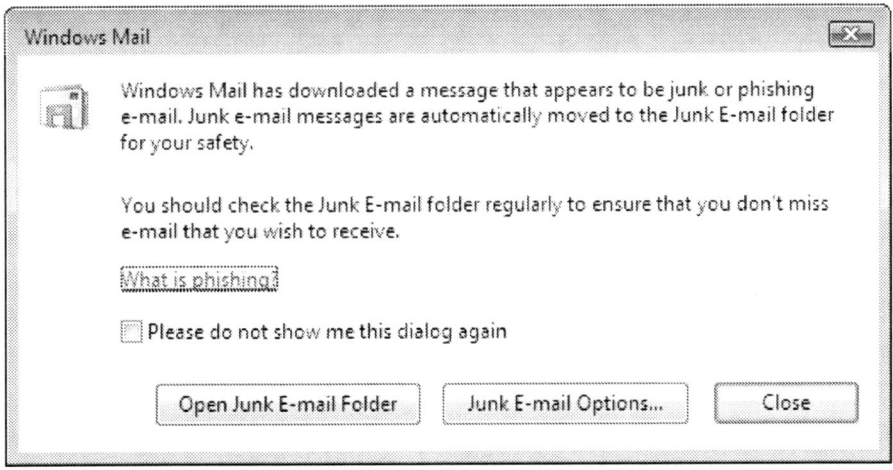

Figure 57 Windows Mail (Junk E-mail Notification)

If that dialog becomes too annoying you can always request it not to be shown, by checking the box labeled **Please do not show me this dialog again**. In reality, you may well run for months or even years without ever receiving any junk messages – providing you don't broadcast your e-mail address carelessly on web sites.

Regardless of your settings, it's a good idea to check your Junk E-mail folder periodically in case any bona fide messages have been wrongly identified as junk. If you find that to be the case, simply add the sender's e-mail address to your Safe Senders List.

Message Rules

Do you remember I told you that, in the early days of the Internet explosion, I used to advertise my e-mail address willy-nilly on web sites? I bet many people do that even now, on the popular social networking sites.

Luckily for me, the e-mail addresses I advertised were those suffixed with my domain name *loton.net*. And the fact that I advertised the e-mail address <u>tony@loton.net</u> does not prevent me from now switching to the e-mail address <u>tonyloton@loton.net</u>.

Unluckily for me, my domain name provider forwards all e-mail ending *loton.net* to a single POP mailbox; so while I can receive messages sent to my new unadvertised e-mail address (<u>tonyloton@loton.net</u>), I can't avoid the messages – the SPAM – sent to my old advertised e-mail address (<u>tony@loton.net</u>). Well, actually I can avoid them. Not at source, but as soon as they land in Windows Mail.

My first step is to create a new folder by right-clicking **Local Folders** and selecting **New Folder...**. I name the new folder *Messages to OLD e-mail address (tony@loton.net)* because I want that folder to hold all of the (potential SPAM) messages sent to my old e-mail address. Figure 58 shows the result so far:

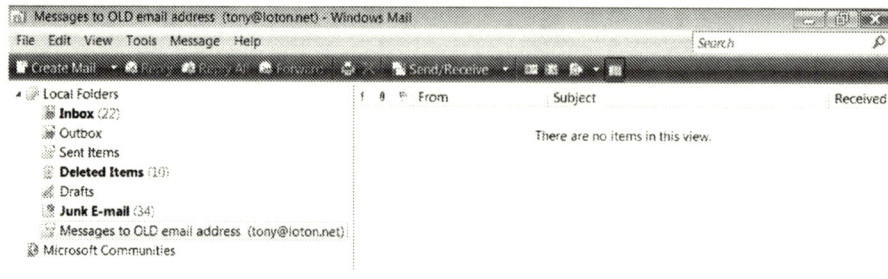

Figure 58 New Folder for messages to old e-mail address

Not only do I want that folder to <u>contain</u> the messages sent to my old e-mail address, but I also want them to be <u>placed there automatically</u>.

To do this I add a message rule by choosing menu option **Tools, Message Rules, Mail**:

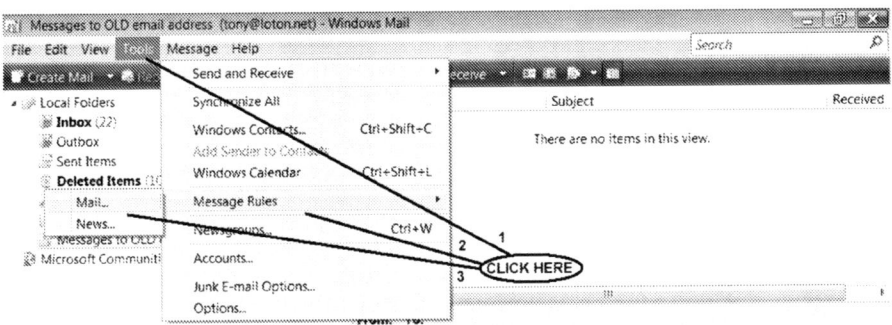

Figure 59 Tools, Message Rules, Mail

Then on the *New Mail Rule* dialog (Figure 60) I select the condition for my rule to be **Where the To line contains people**, and the action for my rule to be **Move it to the specified folder**:

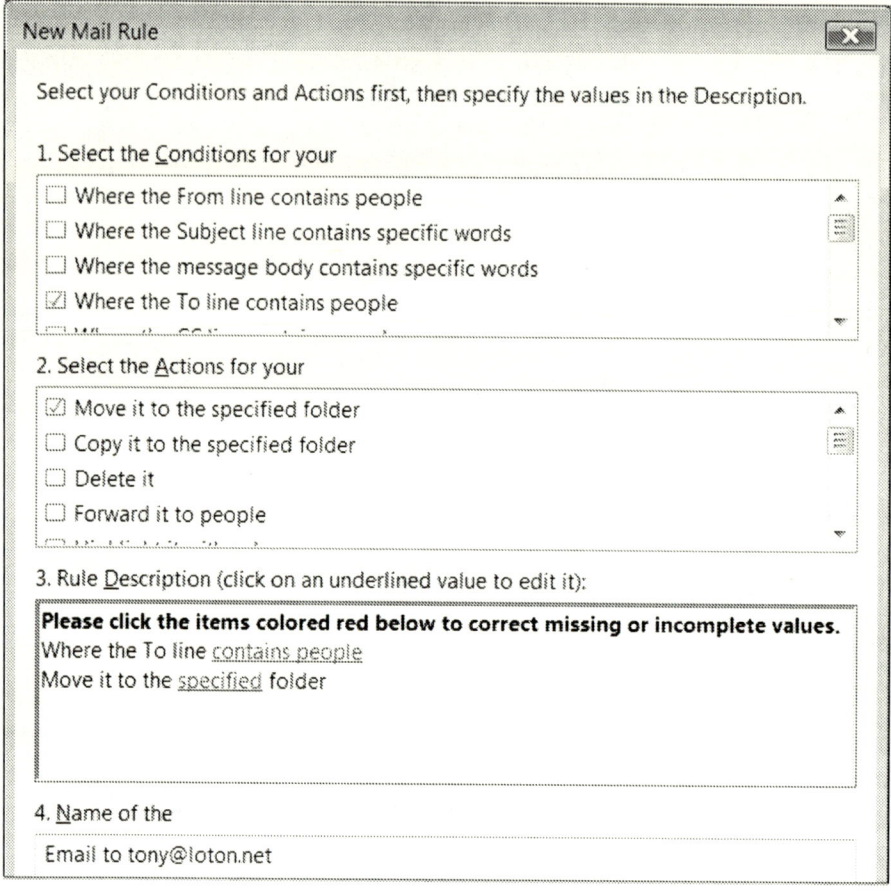

Figure 60 New Mail Rule

Now by clicking the text *Where the To line* **contains people** and the text *Move it to the* **specified** *folder* I can launch the *Select People* and *Move* dialogs in turn.

In the *Select People* dialog (Figure 61) I enter the e-mail address tony@loton.net (my old e-mail address). Messages to this address are the ones I want to redirect.

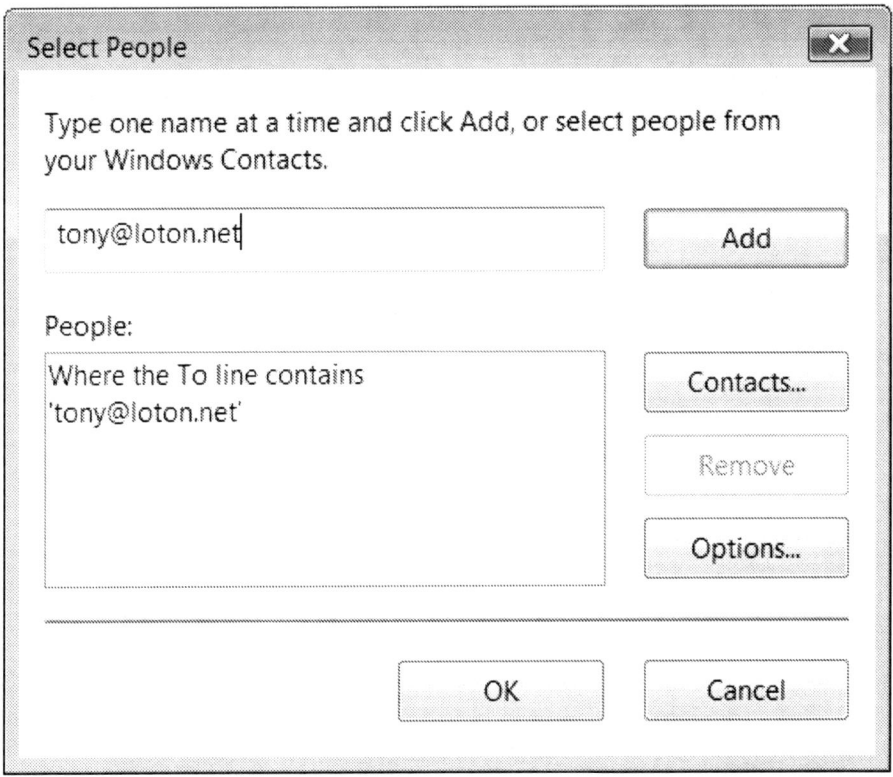

Figure 61 Select People

In the *Move* dialog (Figure 62) I select the new folder that I created, to which I wish the messages to <u>tony@loton.net</u> to be redirected:

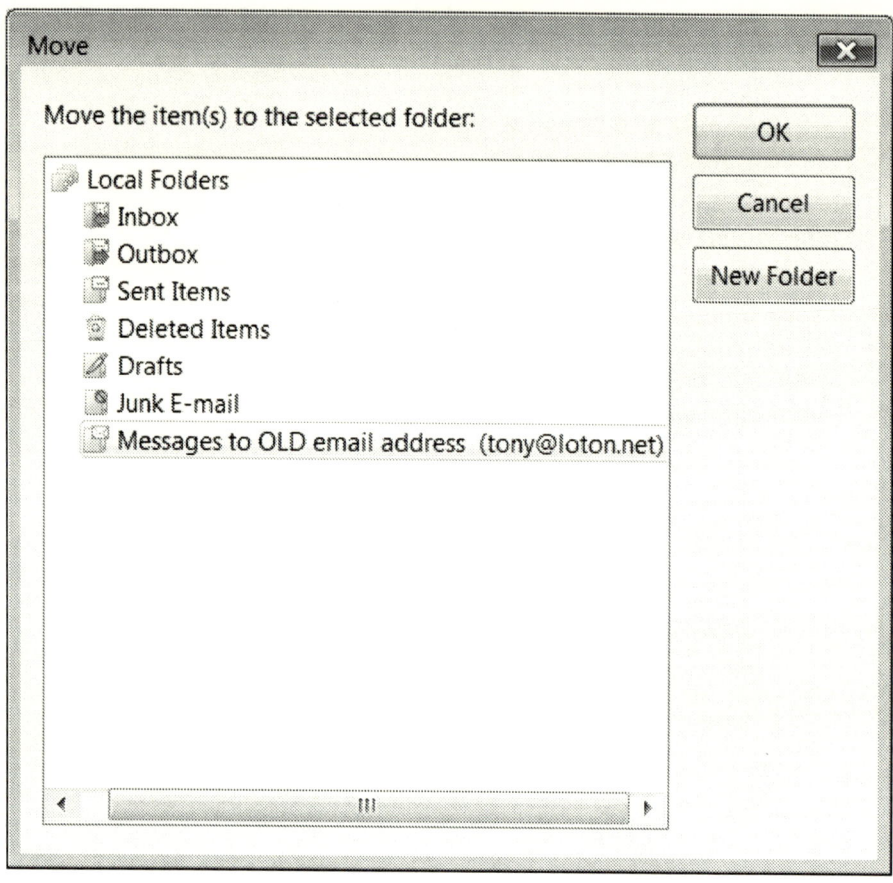

Figure 62 Move

That's all there is to it, and you can see the end result next in Figure 63:

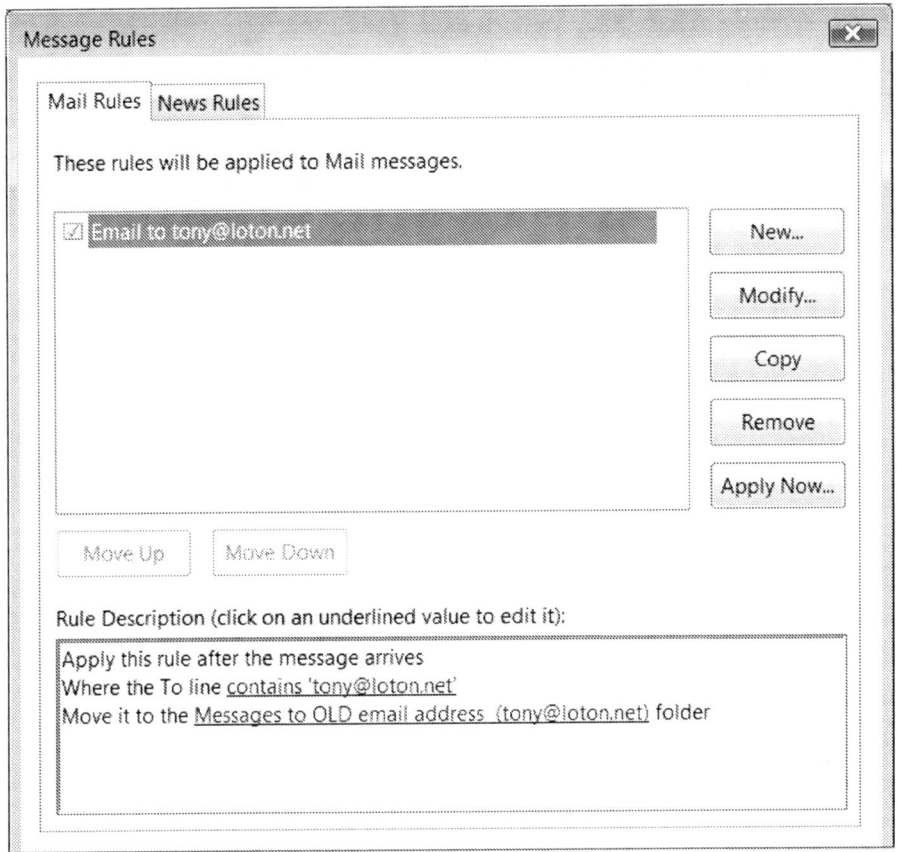

Figure 63 Message Rules dialog, end result

I tested this rule by sending an e-mail message to tony@loton.net and, as expected, when I checked my messages in Windows Mail, this one had found its way into the designated folder automatically.

I know that you or your children probably don't have an old e-mail address from which you'd like to redirect messages in this way, but take a look back at *Figure 60* and think about this more generally. What about setting a message rule that automatically deletes any messages that contain the word "Viagra" on the subject line, before they reach the *In Box*?

Computers Running Windows XP

Any of your computers running the older Windows XP will not have Windows Mail installed. However, they will most likely already have the free Outlook Express e-mail software installed, or the full Microsoft Office Outlook (because you've bought it).

Both products provide the same kinds of features for setting up e-mail accounts, filtering out Junk e-mail, and creating your own message rules.

Alternatively, you might have used a web-based e-mail application that provides similar features. I use Yahoo!Mail which provides SPAM (Junk e-mail) protection, message filtering (like message rules), and disposable e-mail addresses (so that potentially malicious parties need not know your real e-mail address). Check with your web-based e-mail provider for more details.

Summary

By following the steps in this chapter you will have set up Windows Mail to send and receive e-mail for each family member, and filtered the incoming messages to remove unwanted content.

In the next chapter we'll move on from computer configuration techniques, to look at the practices that individual users can adopt in order to protect themselves.

7 – Safe Computing Tips for Users

Objective: To teach computer users how to protect themselves.

The configuration steps outlined in the previous chapters are all well and good, but often the weakest link in the 'safe computing chain' is not the computer and its software at all... but the users themselves. As an analogy: your home might have the most sophisticated security system there is, but it is totally useless if you forget to set the alarm and lock the doors when you go out.

The purpose of this chapter, then, is to outline some of the practical steps that you and your family can take in the quest to stay safe. I follow the same sequence as the prior chapters; that is, I consider practices to adopt when using the computer itself, practices to adopt when browsing the World Wide Web, and finally practices to adopt when using e-mail and other communication facilities.

Before we begin, I'd like to say "Don't Panic!" By its very nature, this chapter focuses on computing dangers rather than benefits. There are many benefits, which is why we all have personal computers in our homes. Take these practices as a way of limiting the risks whilst maximizing the benefits.

Safe Off-line Computing

You might think that safe computing is all about your on-line activities, but it's not. There are some practical steps you can take while computing off-line, to protect your privacy and your data.

Log on to your own user account

Don't be tempted to 'borrow' another family member's username and password to log on with. By always logging on using their own user account: not only will family members have a set of parental controls appropriate to their age group, but also their own user files will be separated from – and protected from the prying eyes of – other family members. As a parent administrator you will always have access to those files, and you will be able to review computing activities on a per-user basis via activity reports.

Backup your files

This one is more important than you think. Trust me.

Many years working as a IT professional and as an end user tells me that <u>you will lose products of your hard work one day</u>; maybe as a result of your own mistakes, for example when you accidentally reformat your hard disk; maybe through no fault of your own, because your computer simply breaks down.

Backing up your files might seem pointless and a little tedious, but the process can be simplified and semi-automated. To get started, you can launch the **Backup and Restore Center** by choosing **All Programs, Maintenance,**

Backup and Restore Center from the Windows Vista **Start** menu.

Locate the family computer in a communal place
While browsing an on-line forum dedicated to safe computing I came across a question from a concerned parent asking...

"How can I prevent my teenage son from accessing pornographic sites on the Internet?"

The expert reply not only suggested that this may be a normal part of growing up, but also suggested that the computer be located in a communal living area with the screen pointing towards the center of the room.

That sounds like a great low-tech solution to a high-tech problem, but I realize it might not always be practical to take children's computers out of their own rooms. Especially if you have six children!

Safe Browsing
The majority of this book has been concerned with protecting family members against potentially malevolent forces on the Internet. While the Windows Vista features go a long way to providing a safe on-line experience, there are some additional practical measures that all users can – and should – take.

Don't give away too much personal information
Many web sites, particularly the social networking sites, encourage you to post personal information on-line. I'm thinking of web sites like MySpace, FaceBook, Bebo, YouTube and the like. And the kind of information I'm thinking about is your name, date of birth, address etc.

There's a theoretical possibility that with enough personal information an identity thief could impersonate you. For minors there are other obvious dangers of posting too much personal information on web sites.

Enter secure information only on Secure Sites

By 'secure information' I mean things like credit card numbers (which could be used fraudulently) and social security numbers (which could be used for identity theft).

That kind of information should only be entered into web sites that you trust such as your bank, the government web site(s), and the major e-commerce sites (like Amazon). And only if the web site is *secure*.

So how do you know if a web site is secure?

First of all, it might say so, but don't believe everything you read. Second, when you visit the 'secure' part of the web site the URL (the web site address, shown in the browser's address bar) should start with **https://** rather than plain old **http://**. Third, a padlock symbol should appear on your web browser.

Use an Internet-only credit card or payment account

Although the majority of credit cards provide a degree of protection against on-line fraud, you can protect yourself further by ordering goods using a credit card that you only use for on-line purchases. You could set a particularly low credit limit on that card.

Another idea would be to not give out your credit card number to web sites at all. Instead, you could open an on-line payment account such as a Paypal account (www.paypal.com), and always use your (PayPal) username to make on-line payments. Only Paypal would know your bank account details or credit card number. But there is a catch, which is that not all web sites accept PayPal.

Use password(s) effectively
When you register with a web site, you will in most cases be asked to choose a password. This usually applies whether you are making a purchase or simply signing up as a user of the web site.

The standard advice is to use a hard-to-guess password (i.e. not your child's name), and to use a different password for every site you use (not so easy). Like me, you might be registered with several banks, e-commerce sites, and social networking sites; which is why choosing – and remembering – a separate password for each one is not so easy.

Let's be realistic about this. You definitely don't want anyone to access your bank account, so bank accounts should always have different passwords. But you might be able to live with the risk that someone who guesses your FaceBook password can therefore – until you report it – gain access to your YouTube account using the same password. To be clear, I'm not recommending you use the same password on multiple sites, but recognizing the fact that you'll need to strike a balance between security and convenience.

Use disposable e-mail addresses
Most web sites that you register with will ask for your e-mail address, and many will insist on this being used as your username. In the fullness of time you will receive unsolicited junk e-mail (or SPAM) to the e-mail address you provide on-line.

It is therefore a good idea to never give out your main e-mail address in this way. There are plenty of free e-mail providers

– such as Google, Yahoo! – with whom you can set up a second e-mail address to use on-line.

Alternatively, your main e-mail provider may well provide a facility for setting up additional 'disposable' e-mail addresses that hang off your main address. My e-mail provider, BTYahoo!, allows me to set up disposable e-mail addresses using a feature named AddressGuard.

Regardless of how you get your second e-mail address, the point is that you can stop using it once it becomes overwhelmed with SPAM. Just set up another address and start using that one instead.

Safe E-mail
The tip just described is related to e-mail, but specifically to the use of e-mail addresses on web sites. I have a few more tips on how to use e-mail safely, these tips also being applicable to other communication facilities such as Instant Messaging.

Don't send sensitive information by e-mail
E-mail messages are sent as plain text or HTML, unencrypted; which means that your message may be read in transit by anyone sophisticated enough to intercept it.

For that reason you should never include sensitive personal information in an e-mail message. Order numbers for your on-line purchases should be ok, but not your credit card number nor your social security number.

You might even notice that some organizations routinely strip out sensitive information from e-mail messages, for your protection. I recently received a reply to a query that I submitted to Her Majesty's Revenue and Customs (HMRC, the UK tax office) suffixed with the following paragraph:

For security reasons specific personal data may have been removed from this e-mail.

If they don't think it's safe, nor should you.

Don't open attachments from unknown sources
Viruses, spyware, and other malicious programs are often sent as e-mail attachments. So if you receive an e-mail with an attachment from someone you don't know, don't open the attachment no matter how alluring it sounds.

Don't click links in e-mail messages
A common technique used by fraudsters these days is *phishing*. You are sent an e-mail purporting to be, for example, from you bank; the e-mail inviting you to click a link to visit their web site so as to update your security details.

It looks very plausible, as does the web site at the end of the link, but it's just a very clever copy of your bank's own web site.

Of course, your bank will have given you a bona fide link to their on-line banking website when you signed up, for example http://banking.mybank.com. So, if you receive an e-mail containing that exact link it should be ok. Shouldn't it?

Actually no; because the text you see in the e-mail is just descriptive text describing the link, which need not match the link address itself. Put simply, a link labeled http://banking.mybank.com might actually lead you to http://phishing.fraudsters.com. If in doubt, copy the link text that you trust (http://banking.mybank.com) and paste it into the web browsers address bar – to make sure that's where you go.

Don't reply to unsolicited messages

If you receive an unsolicited e-mail message, do not be tempted to reply to it, even to ask for removal from the mailing list. The chances are that you will not be removed from the list and you will merely have confirmed that your e-mail address is 'live' (i.e. being read).

Disguise your e-mail address

In the early days of the World Wide Web I was very keen to promote my wares on my company's web site. Good citizen that I am, I provided a contact e-mail address for customers.

Some years on, I now receive more SPAM e-mails than genuine ones to that e-mail address; in fact, a ratio of about 20-to-1. That's because sophisticated spammers have computer programs that scan the world's web pages automatically looking for candidate e-mail addresses. For that reason, you may well see contact e-mail addresses now listed in a format that a human can recognize more easily than a computer program; with instructions on how to determine the real e-mail address. Like this:

```
Please contact me at "tonyATlotonDOTnet"

(Don't forget to replace the word AT with @ and the
word DOT with '.')
```

Though you might not have your own web site, there's a good chance that you will include your e-mail address in a forum posting, or on a social networking site. All the better, then, to do it in a disguised way.

Summary

By adopting the practices outlined in this chapter, computer users can strengthen the weakest link in the safe computing chain... themselves.

Appendix A – Windows XP Family Safety

Objective: To provide Vista-like parental controls on Windows XP computers.

Computers running the older Windows XP operating system are not equipped with the parental controls functionality that is present in Windows Vista. At various points in this book I have suggested some Windows XP alternative solutions, and in most cases also mentioned the availability of a Microsoft solution named Windows Live OneCare.

Windows Live OneCare not only provides an antivirus facility, which is absent even in Windows Vista, but also a parental controls feature that equips Windows XP with the same family safety features that are present in Vista.

The purpose of this appendix is not to provide a blow-by-blow account of how to download, install, and sign up for the software; but merely to make you aware of its existence and point you in the right direction.

Visit http://get.live.com/familysafety/features and you will see this web page:

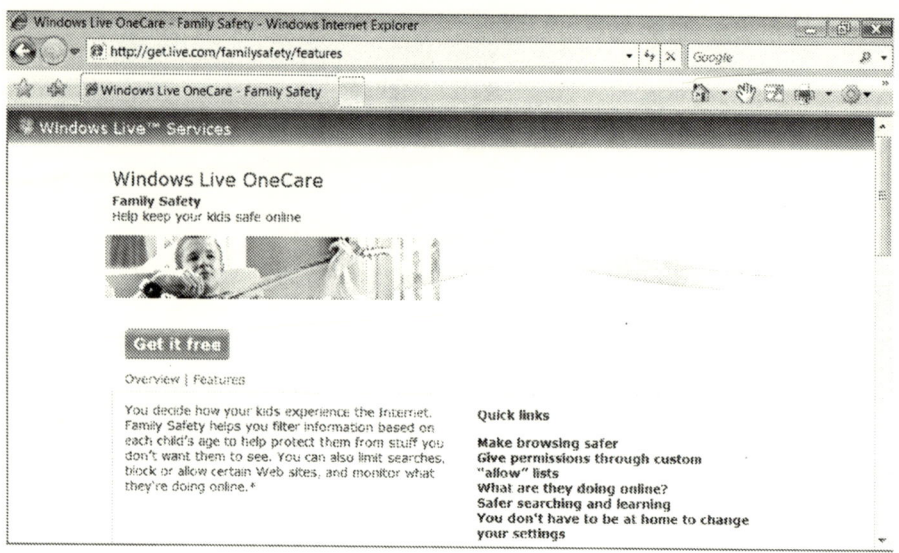

Figure 64 Windows Live OneCare – Family Safety

To get started, you'll have to click the **Get it free** button. You'll need to create a Windows Live ID, if you don't already have one, as part of the process.

Rather than clicking the **Get it free** button, in the following figure I have scrolled down the page to give you an idea of what is included.

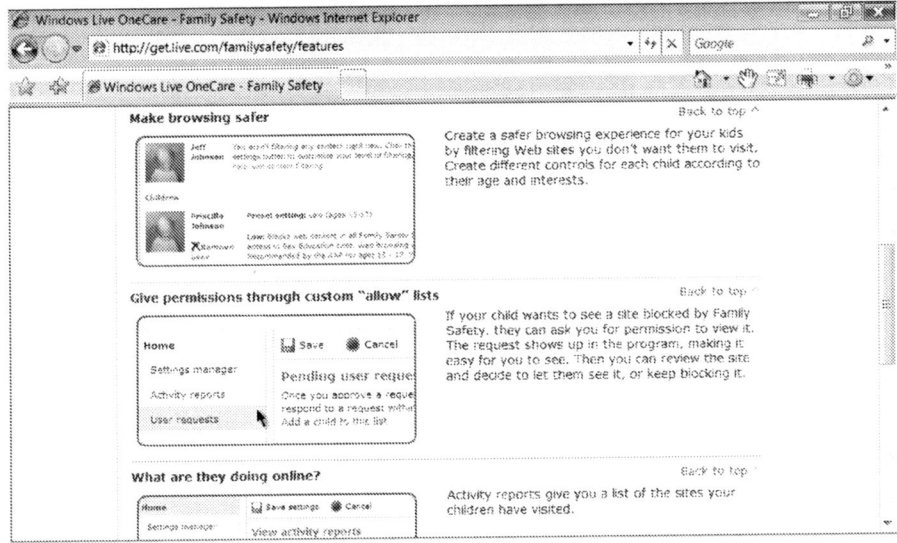

Figure 65 Windows Live OneCare – Family Safety, scroll down

Here you can see a way to *Make browsing safer* (like Vista web restrictions), a way to *Give permissions through custom "allow" lists* (also a function of Vista web restrictions), and a way to find out *What are they doing online?* (like Vista activity reports).

Also by this author

Tony Loton's IT and finance books published by LOTONtech are available at www.lotontech.com and www.lulu.com/lotontech.

Tony's previous IT books published by John Wiley & Sons and Wrox Press are available from the Wiley website at www.wiley.com. Those books are:

Professional Visual Studio 2005 Team System, ISBN 978-0764584367

Professional UML with Visual Studio .NET, ISBN 978-0764543760

Web Content Mining with Java, ISBN 978-0470843116

Index

Printed in the United Kingdom by
Lightning Source UK Ltd., Milton Keynes
141695UK00001B/238/A